LONDON
&
The Famous

**AN HISTORICAL GUIDE TO
FIFTY FAMOUS PEOPLE AND THEIR LONDON HOMES**

LONDON
&
The Famous

AN HISTORICAL GUIDE TO
FIFTY FAMOUS PEOPLE AND THEIR LONDON HOMES

Katy Carter

Photographs by
**Helen Douglas-Cooper
and Sandy Young**

British Tourist Authority
London

First published in 1982
by the British Tourist Authority,
4 Bromells Road, London SW4 0BJ

Copyright © Swallow Publishing Limited 1982
Photographs copyright © Helen Douglas-Cooper and Sandy Young
Originated by Swallow Publishing Limited

ISBN 0-70950-938-3

Printed in Great Britain
by The Pitman Press, Bath

Contents

Preface

James Boswell once said: 'I have often amused myself with thinking how different a place London is to different people', and no reader of this book is likely to disagree with him. From Thomas Hardy, to whom the city was 'a monster with four million heads and eight million eyes', to Doctor Johnson, for whom 'when a man is tired of London, he is tired of life, for there is in London all that life can afford', the fifty famous ex-residents of London covered in this book held widely diverging views on the city which, at some stage in their lives, they made their home.

My aim in this book has been to trace the links between London and some of its erstwhile residents by concentrating on their London homes. It is hard to define the fascination of being able to say: 'So-and-so lived here'; but whatever it is, there is a unique historical *frisson* to be gained from, for instance, standing on the pavement outside the house in which Mozart wrote his first symphony at the age of eight, or actually standing inside the attic where Johnson compiled his great *Dictionary*. With this in mind, I have concentrated on discovering what part a house (or houses) played in its occupant's life, and on his or her experiences in London while living there, while giving background biographical details where it seems useful.

Given the fact that these fifty people between them witnessed some three hundred years of London's history, the diversity of their experiences in and reactions to London is hardly surprising. The London Hardy saw, in the late nineteenth century, was very different from Johnson's mid-eighteenth century metropolis: the expansion of the suburbs, the coming of the railways and industrialization were all unrealized in Johnson's time, but facts of life in Hardy's. While Johnson's contemporaries complained frequently about the constant threat of highway robbery, nineteenth century Londoners were more likely to protest about the appalling industrial smog which wrapped up London 'like a mummy', in the words of Elizabeth Browning.

Indeed, it is not easy for us to envisage how much London must have altered in three hundred years. No one that long ago would even have used the word London to describe the huge urban area which we now call by that name for convenience: each part of 'London' was distinct, each community growing and developing in its own way and acquiring a character which to some extent is still evident today. Take Chelsea, for instance: three hundred years ago it was, Macaulay noted, a 'quiet country village, with about a thousand inhabitants, the baptisms averaging little more than forty in the year', and it was separated from Westminster by the marshy Five Fields, notorious for their highwaymen. By the end of the eighteenth century, however, it had become more of a town than a village: it had acquired a new respectability, and 'many honourable and worthy inhabitants' were attracted by its riverside situation, a calm and pleasant retreat from bustling Westminster. Ranelagh pleasure gardens, the Botanical Gardens and Don Saltero's coffee-house in Cheyne Walk were the places where the fashionable were to be seen. But by 1833, Macaulay noted that Chelsea had become 'proverbial for its dulness' though 'formerly a place of great gaiety', and only at the end of the nineteenth century did it become the acknowledged quarter for artists and writers, by which time the land between Chelsea and Westminster had been built up, and the Five Fields were no more. Many such changes are observed incidentally in the following pages.

The choice of fifty men and women from a potential cast of thousands has necessarily been somewhat arbitrary. In many cases, the houses of those chosen bear the blue plaques erected by the Greater London Council or by its predecessors the London County Council or the Royal Society of Arts (there are now some four hundred of these plaques in total). Others are included whom the G.L.C. has passed by or whose deaths have occurred too recently for the G.L.C. to start considering whether their achievements deserve a permanent memorial. The first criterion has been that the houses are still standing (with one exception, that of Boswell) and substantially as they were at the time of the famous resident. Secondly, most of the characters chosen are very well known and likely to need little introduction. Thirdly, I have included a high proportion of foreigners, whose connections with London may not be generally known: Marx, Handel and Henry James may be well known as Londoners, but how many people are,aware that Canaletto spent some years in London, churning out views of the city by the score for the tourist trade? Finally, all those whose London homes are preserved as museums open to the public have been included (opening times are given in the text).

Many of the houses mentioned in this book are in central London; the others are scattered further afield in Greater London, for the benefit of the Londoner or perhaps the more adventurous tourist. Many of the houses are relatively modest establishments, by no means among the 'architectural landmarks' of London; but, from the grandeur of Wellington's Apsley House standing serenely on Hyde Park Corner to the anonymity of the two first-floor rooms in a humble terrace in Kennington where Charlie Chaplin spent part of his childhood, each has its unique fascination.

Robert Adam (1728–92)

1–3 Robert Street, WC2

Very little now remains in London of the work of Robert Adam, whose rejection of the rigid architectural rules of Palladianism in the mid eighteenth century brought a fresh and exciting face to London's architecture.

The Adelphi Terrace

But from prints and drawings made at the time, and from the fragments which remain, including 1–3 Robert Street, it is still possible to imagine the splendour of the Adelphi Terrace, built by the brothers Adam (hence the name Adelphi, which is the Greek word for brothers) from 1768–74. The project, which gave them their only opportunity in central London to build on the grand scale to which they were accustomed in Scotland, was bold in conception and design; Robert Adam planned to construct a building on the banks of the Thames to echo the grandeur of the ruined Palace of Diocletian at Spalato, which he so much admired. The chosen site, leased to the brothers by the Duke of St Albans, was, before work commenced, nothing but a muddy slope down from the Strand to the water's edge (the Thames then had not been embanked). The plan was to build a row of houses

Tube: Charing Cross.
Bus: Nos. 1, 6, 9, 11, 13, 15, 77, 168, 170, 172, 176.

The Adelphi Terrace, as it looked when it was first built. *(St Martin's Prints)*

upon a riverside terrace supported on great arches, to bring the houses to the level of the Strand — in effect, the first attempt to embank the Thames architecturally.

The brothers faced the ridicule of many contemporaries, constant financial difficulties, and the obstructiveness of vested interests, who forced the brothers to obtain an Act of Parliament to enclose and embank part of the river. But despite this, the Terrace and the streets behind it which linked it to the Strand (Adam Street and Robert Street at either end being the most important) were completed in 1774. The finished building, standing secure on its brick vaults, was gaily embellished with fluted pilasters and other ornamentation. The whole was characteristic of Adam's innovative style, which again brought criticism from conservatives, notably Horace Walpole (never one to be sparing in his criticism) who protested 'What are the Adelphi Buildings? warehouses laced down the seams, like a soldier's trill in a regimental lace coat.' And in fact, few people bought the houses which the Adam brothers had anticipated no difficulty in selling, even though David Garrick, a good friend, set an example by moving in immediately. Part of his drawing room, designed by Robert Adam, can now be seen in the Victoria and Albert Museum. Not surprisingly, bankruptcy loomed, and with a touch of panache to match their style of architecture the brothers held a lottery — again sanctioned by Act of Parliament — to sell the houses, causing Horace Walpole to scorn 'What patronage of the arts in Parliament, to vote the City's land to these brothers, and then sanctify the sale of the houses by a bubble!' But the ploy was successful, and the brothers remained solvent.

The fate of the Adelphi

The Adelphi was never a great success in any way other than architecturally, though it attracted some illustrious residents over the years, including Thomas Hardy and George Bernard Shaw, and housed the original premises of such diverse institutions as the London School of Economics and the Savage Club. It was finally demolished in 1936, although, as John Summerson argues in *Georgian London*, it was effectively destroyed when the exterior was remodelled in 1872; at any rate its effect was muted by the building of the Victoria Embankment roadway and gardens in 1864–70. Of the fragments now remaining, those which best illustrate the original appearance are the only surviving house, no. 7 Adam Street, and also the building in John Adam Street which was expressly built for the Royal Society of Arts, and which has a fine entrance hall designed by Robert Adam. No. 3 Robert Street has been altered, but is the only surviving fragment of the Adelphi river elevation, and it was here that Robert Adam and his brother James lived from 1778.

Nos. 1-3 Robert Street,
one of the few remaining
fragments of the Adelphi.

Adam's works

The other remaining buildings, unfortunately few and far between,
designed by Robert Adam in London, can give an idea of how the
Adelphi once looked. The finest, Chandos House in Chandos
Street, 20 St James's Square, and Home House, 20 Portman
Square, all show the lightness of touch which distinguished his
art from the rather sombre style of his contemporaries, and one
can also still admire the grace of his Admiralty Screen, constructed 1759–61. At Home House, now the Courtauld Institute
of Art, there is a particularly fine staircase designed by Adam
(the interior of the building may be visited in vacations).

One has to go a little further afield best to appreciate Adam's
fine interior designs, and his talent for making architecture serve
the needs of social life. This can be observed at Syon House, at
Osterley Park, and nearer at hand, at Kenwood House in Highgate.
At Kenwood, Adam was allowed by Lord Mansfield 'full scope
for my ideas', as he had been at the Adelphi, in both exterior and
interior design, and the result was a masterpiece which may still
be admired today.

Hector Berlioz (1803–69)

58 Queen Anne Street, W1

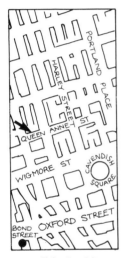

Tube: Bond Street.
Bus: Nos. 3, 53, 137.

58 Queen Anne Street,
where Berlioz stayed
during the Great
Exhibition of 1851

The French composer Berlioz visited London five times. His first
visit was in 1847–48, at the invitation of Jullien, the Director of
the Grand English Opera Company of Drury Lane, who asked
Berlioz to come and conduct for the company for six years. That
visit turned out to be disastrous, since Jullien went bankrupt,
and Berlioz, who had been staying in Jullien's house at 27 Harley
Street, found himself turned out by the bailiffs!

The next visit, in 1851, was less dramatic. It was on this

occasion that Berlioz stayed at 58 Queen Anne Street, having been chosen by the French authorities to be a member of the committee of judges of musical instruments at the Great Exhibition in London in that year.

When Berlioz arrived in London, the city was packed with visitors to the Exhibition. Prophets of doom were convinced that Prince Albert's grandiose scheme was a complete folly, and that the number of foreigners and unruly provincials descending on London would cause 'confusion, disorder and demoralization, if not actual revolution . . . famine and pestilence'. But the Exhibition, which opened in May, was an amazing success: over six million people flocked to the Crystal Palace, the towering edifice of glass and iron built in Hyde Park for the occasion, and with the profits from the Exhibition were built many of the museums, concert halls and other cultural institutions which now grace South Kensington.

Out of tune

But for Berlioz, the Exhibition proved to be a tedious business, even though his lodgings in Queen Anne Street, Marylebone, were reasonably close to Hyde Park. Day after day he performed 'the stupid job of examining the musical instruments'. 'It splits your head to hear these hundreds of wretched machines, each more out of tune than the next.' The Exhibition halls were always packed —it was estimated that there were often 100,000 people there at any one time — and only if he arrived early in the morning did he get any peace. But Berlioz stayed doggedly on until the end of the Exhibition in July, by which time all the other French judges had packed their bags and left, 'in order to see justice done . . . France comes out ahead beyond any possible comparison . . . The rest is more or less in the class of penny whistles and pots and pans'.

Still, there were compensations. Berlioz wrote during his visit that 'There is no city in the world, I am convinced, where so much music is consumed as in London' and he did not have to go far to hear it. The house in which he was staying belonged to a Professor of Music, and contained the famous New Beethoven Rooms, where the Beethoven Quartet Society gave frequent concerts. To his delight Berlioz discovered: 'My apartment being situated above the main staircase, I could easily hear the whole performance by simply opening my door.'

Berlioz returned to London in 1852, 1853 and 1855, having been invited over to conduct concerts. He always stayed in the Marylebone area, then as now part of the fashionable West End, and which had been urbanized comparatively recently, during the eighteenth century. The Queen Anne Street house, a Georgian building with early Victorian trimmings and little altered since 1851, was chosen to bear a plaque as it is the only one of Berlioz's London residences which is still standing.

William Bligh (1754–1817)

100 Lambeth Road, SE1

Tube: Lambeth North or Waterloo.
Bus: Nos. 3, 10, 44, 109, 155, 159, 172.

The ordinary three-storey terraced house in Lambeth Road bought by William Bligh in 1794 betrays no sign of its former owner's turbulent life.

Born in Cornwall in 1754, William Bligh had accompanied Captain Cook on his second world voyage in the *Resolution* in 1772–74. This voyage led to Bligh's appointment to the *Bounty* in 1787. As on Cook's voyage the bread-fruit was first discovered by the English at Otaheite, Bligh's task was to introduce the plant to the West Indies. At the end of the year, Bligh and his crew sailed in the *Bounty* for Otaheite, and stopped there for six months before setting off for the West Indies. The story of the ensuing mutiny has become a legend. Shortly after leaving Otaheite the crew, led by the master's mate Fletcher Christian, mutinied, and cast Bligh and eighteen loyal crew members adrift in an open boat. The mutineers made for Pitcairn Island, where they settled (and where their descendants live to the present day). William Bligh and his companions, after drifting for 4000 miles and suffering badly from exposure, thirst and hunger, eventually landed at Timor.

Returning to England in 1790, Bligh was vindicated of any blame for the mutiny in the court martial which investigated the loss of the ship, and his account of the troubles, published as *A Voyage to the South Sea, undertaken by command of His Majesty, for the Purpose of Conveying the Bread-Fruit Tree to the West Indies*, was a great success. The following year he sailed on a second 'bread-fruit' expedition, this time completing his earlier mission to introduce the fruit to the West Indies. On his return, Bligh moved with his wife and family to a new house in Lambeth: 3 Durham Place (now 100 Lambeth Road).

Further troubles

Bligh's career continued to be turbulent. After a successful period as a naval commander, in 1805 he was appointed Captain General and Governor of New South Wales. He left his wife and younger children at the house in Lambeth and sailed with his daughter and son-in-law to Australia in February 1806. Once again, his temperament, courageous and honest but also fiery

100 Lambeth Road

and authoritarian, stirred up violent feelings against him, and in January 1808 he was again the centre of a mutiny, this time led by an infantry officer, Major George Johnston. Bligh was imprisoned by the mutineers, and was not freed until 1810.

His wife, meanwhile, remained at Lambeth. Throughout their marriage, their relationship seems to have been loving and affectionate, a revealing glimpse into Bligh's character, and one which seems to contradict the legend that Bligh was cruel and vindictive, and hence totally to blame for the mutiny on the *Bounty*. A letter, written from Durham Place and dated August 1808 still exists: it was sent by Bligh's wife Elizabeth to her imprisoned husband, along with a box containing provisions, clothes and newspapers. The letter ends:

> . . . this box I hope you will receive safe with my most sincere and affectionate Love. The Dear Children send their affectionate Duty — And I am, my dear Mr Bligh most sincerely your Elizabeth Bligh.

The New South Wales mutiny was overcome in 1810 and in 1811 Bligh returned once more to Durham Place and his family. Another court martial ensued, and Bligh's wife, perhaps unable to take the strain of this, died in 1812 at Durham Place. Deeply distressed and embittered by his experiences, Bligh moved from London to a house at Farningham, Kent, and lived there quietly until his death in 1817. He was buried alongside his wife in the churchyard of St Mary's, Lambeth, where his tomb may be seen.

James Boswell (1740–95)

122 Great Portland Street, W1

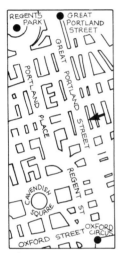

Tube: Great Portland Street.
Bus: Nos. 3, 53, 137.

It is a surprising fact about Boswell that he spent most of his life not in London, as his close connection with Dr Johnson might suggest, but in Edinburgh, where for most of his career Boswell was in legal practice. However, he visited London regularly almost every spring, chiefly for the purpose of seeing Johnson and the pleasure of mixing with other convivial companions. Though Edinburgh was a lively city, experiencing its cultural Golden Age, to Boswell it could not be compared to London, which, he professed, was 'the best place when one is happy', but 'equally so when one is the reverse'.

Boswell's first visit to London was in 1760, when his purpose was to be accepted into the Roman Catholic Church. However, when he arrived, the hitherto celibate youth rapidly found the pleasures of the flesh more attractive than vows of religion, and furthermore decided he would prefer to join the Guards rather than enter the legal profession as his father Lord Auchinleck intended. His father, rather alarmed, summoned him back to Edinburgh as soon as possible.

Sightseeing

The young Boswell, eager for adventure, was back in London, where he took lodgings in Downing Street, in November 1762, staying until August of the following year, and kept a lively account of the visit in his *London Journal*. He kept himself fairly busy, entertaining girls picked up in the street, watching public executions, and visiting taverns. Occasionally he would find time for more conventional sightseeing, as on one occasion when he decided to climb the 311 steps of the Monument, erected to commemorate the Great Fire. Despite great trepidation, he managed to reach the top, where he dared not look down, fearing that the traffic below shaking the ground 'would make the tremendous pile tumble to the foundation'.

Boswell meets Johnson

It was also on this visit that Boswell first met Samuel Johnson, in the back room of Thomas Davies' bookshop in Russell Street.

An eighteenth century engraving of the Monument. *(Reproduced by kind permission of Robert Douwma Prints & Maps Ltd, London)*

Johnson on this occasion rather poured scorn on Boswell's nervous attempts to flatter him, but was welcoming when Boswell summoned up the courage to visit Johnson at his chambers in the Inner Temple. A firm friendship was rapidly established, and Johnson was so taken with the young Boswell that he accompanied him on the four-day journey to Harwich, whence Boswell set off for Holland to further his legal studies.

After a highly successful tour of Europe, which included his six week tour of Corsica resulting in *An Account of Corsica* (1768), the essay which brought him some fame as a writer, Boswell returned to Edinburgh in 1766, passed his examinations in Scots law, and eventually married the only woman with whom he had maintained a lasting friendship, his cousin Margaret Montgomerie, in 1769. Edinburgh remained the scene of Boswell's

122 Great Portland Street

regular professional life until 1786.

'The whole of human life'

However, he looked forward almost feverishly to the visits he made to London nearly every spring: in contrast to the 'supine indolence of mind' from which he felt that he suffered in Edinburgh, when in London 'the intellectual man is struck with it as comprehending the whole of human life in all its variety, the contemplation of which is inexhaustible'. Boswell was so greatly enamoured of London that Johnson felt obliged to write urging him to have a little more care for his wife, always left behind in Edinburgh, and who suffered from consumption. 'I wish' Johnson wrote in July 1778, 'you would a little correct or restrain your imagination, and imagine that happiness, such as life admits, may be had at other places as well as London.'

It was not until 1786, over a year after Johnson's death, that Boswell had his way, and he and his family moved to London permanently. They took a house (now demolished) in Great Queen Street, Lincoln's Inn Fields, the first proper residence Boswell had had in London after a series of widely scattered lodgings. Boswell was now spending much of his time collecting together information for the *Life of Johnson*, published in May 1791.

Last years

But aside from this crowning achievement, Boswell's last years in London were not happy. Bereft of his two great supports, his friend Johnson in 1784 and his patient, forgiving wife in 1789, Boswell, who had always been prone to fits of chronic depression, went into a sad decline. He never really managed to establish himself in legal practice in London as he had intended, and his attempts to satisfy his long-held political ambitions with the help of the notorious boroughmonger Sir James Lowther ended ignominiously. In January 1791 he moved to 122 Great Portland Street, then rather a squalid and insignificant little street, where he forced himself to continue work on the *Life*, and though the work was well received, its author was widely ridiculed: 'I was in truth in a woeful state of depression in every respect.' Though he still sought convivial company, he was no longer regarded as the wit who enlivened any social occasion, and resorted frequently to drink. He died at the house in Great Portland Street on 19 May 1795. (The actual house in which he lived is no longer standing, but a plaque has been erected on a building on its site.)

Elizabeth Barrett Browning (1806–61)

99 Gloucester Place, W1

There are two plaques commemorating the poetess Elizabeth Barrett Browning in London, both in Marylebone: the first at 99 (formerly 74) Gloucester Place and the second at 50 Wimpole Street. The latter plaque only marks the site of a house in which Miss Barrett lived, but Wimpole Street is of course famous for its association with the Barretts, and the name of the street figures in the title of the famous play about the Browning love story.

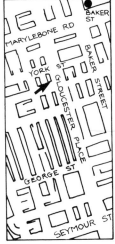

Passive city

No. 99 Gloucester Place, a large, late Georgian building faced with yellow brick, was the first house to which the Barretts moved in London: they came here from Sidmouth, Devon, in 1835, when Elizabeth was twenty-nine. Invalided at the age of fifteen after a riding accident, she spent most of her time indoors. Her impressions of London were not very favourable: 'Was there anybody in the world who ever loved London for itself?' she wondered. 'London is wrapped up like a mummy, in a yellow mist, so closely that I have had scarcely a glimpse of its countenance since we came' she wrote in her first letter from Gloucester Place. Her moody reflections on the city were later recorded in a poem written at Gloucester Place. She describes how she watched the sun

Tube: Baker Street.
Bus: Nos. 1, 2, 13, 30, 74, 113, 159.

> Push out through fog with his dilated disk
> And startle the slant roofs and chimney pots
> With splashes of fierce colour. Or I saw
> Fog only, the great tawny weltering fog,
> Involve the passive city, strangle it
> Alive, and draw it off into the void,
> Spires, bridges, streets and squares, as if a sponge
> Had wiped out London.

Mr Barrett had brought his family to London chiefly to advance his sons' careers (in which he seems to have been successful) but the air did little for Elizabeth's health.

However, she found compensation in the London literary world, into which she was now introduced by John Kenyon, who as a distant relative of the Barretts was one of the few visitors considered acceptable by Elizabeth's father. Well known for his

99 Gloucester Place, the Barretts' first home in London

role as a 'middle-man' of letters, Kenyon introduced Elizabeth to the authoress Mary Russell Mitford, with whom she began a lasting friendship, and through him she also met Wordsworth twice — 'I was not at all disappointed in Wordsworth' she wrote, 'although perhaps I should not have singled him out from the multitude as a great man.' Kenyon also helped her to have many of her poems printed in literary periodicals, which encouraged her to collect together some of her poems for a book, *The Seraphim*, published in 1838.

Move

This book came out after the family had moved from Gloucester Place, however: the Barretts had only intended this to be a temporary home, though in the event they stayed there for three years. Elizabeth was not happy about this, as she wrote to a friend in 1836:

50 Wimpole Street (now demolished), where Elizabeth lived from 1838 until her marriage to Robert Browning

> I had wished very much to have been able to tell you in this letter where we had taken our house, or where we were going to take it. We remain, however, in our usual state of conscious ignorance, although there is a good deal of talking and walking about a house in Wimpole Street, — which between ourselves I am not very anxious to live in, on account of the gloominess of that street . . . Nevertheless, if it is decided upon, I daresay I shall contrive to be satisfied with it, and sleep and wake very much as I should in any other. It will certainly be a point gained to be settled somewhere, and I do so long to sit in my own armchair — strange as it will look out of my own room — and to read from my own books.

In the event, they did move, in the spring of 1838, to the house at no. 50 Wimpole Street; the 'gloominess' of Wimpole Street is now much altered, as the street has been extensively rebuilt since 1900. No. 50 was demolished in 1936.

Here Elizabeth lived for eight years, until her marriage to Robert Browning in 1846. She described her bedroom at Wimpole Street, in which she was usually confined, as a prison — but it was here, eventually, that Robert Browning came to visit her, after a long correspondence, despite her protests: 'There is nothing to see in me, nor to hear in me.' Strangely, Mr Barrett seems not to have objected to Browning's frequent visits, perhaps because he considered Elizabeth now too old and unattractive to form or invite any romantic attachment. It was only his refusal to allow Elizabeth to go with Robert to Italy in 1846 for her health that impelled the couple to take desperate steps. They married secretly at St Marylebone Parish Church, Marylebone Road, where a window commemorates the event, and left for Italy.

The Brownings spent most of their time thereafter in Florence, only revisiting England occasionally. After Elizabeth's death in Florence in 1861 Robert returned, and finally settled in De Vere Gardens, W8, where Henry James was also a resident. He died in Venice in 1889.

Isambard Kingdom Brunel (1806–59)

98 Cheyne Walk, SW10

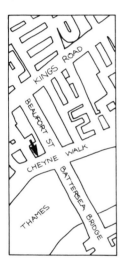

Tube: South Kensington.
Bus: Nos. 11, 19, 22, 39, 45, 49.

Cheyne Walk, which housed a cluster of illustrious artists and writers along its length in the course of the nineteenth century, was also the childhood home of the engineer and visionary Isambard Kingdom Brunel. His father Marc, himself a brilliant engineer, had fled from his native France during the Revolution, settling in Plymouth where he designed and supervised the manufacture of machines to produce ship blocks for the Navy's defence against Napoleon.

The village of palaces

In 1806, shortly after the birth of Isambard, his only son, Marc Brunel moved with his family to London where they took a house, no. 4 Lindsey Row (now 98 Cheyne Walk). This house, which has a beautifully preserved seventeenth century façade and is now owned by the National Trust, has a long and fascinating history. No. 98 forms the central portion of what was once a single three-storey house, built in 1674 by Charles II's Lord Great Chamberlain, Lord Lindsey. The fine mansion, which replaced an earlier palace built by Sir Theodore Mayerne, physician to James I, on the site of what had once been the dwelling and farm of Thomas More, is a reminder that Chelsea had been known since the reign of Henry VIII as a 'village of palaces'. In the eighteenth century the house came into the hands of Count Zinzendorf, who made it the headquarters of the Moravian Church, the brethren who had some influence on the Methodists. In 1775 the house was converted into seven separate dwellings, collectively renamed nos. 1–7 Lindsey Row. No. 4 was given the name Lindsey House by the artist John Martin, who lived there after the Brunels.

By some accounts the builders who converted the old palace were as incompetent as some of their present-day counterparts, thoughtlessly removing the building's distinctive cupolas and balustrade. The portion occupied by the Brunels, however, was the finest, as it contained the original magnificent staircase and lofty, spacious rooms. There were two drawing-rooms on the first floor overlooking the river and garden, bedrooms on the second floor and two attic rooms above for the servants. Marc Brunel made some alterations to the house which were of a functional, rather than aesthetic, nature: he took out the front windows and replaced them with smaller ones using single sheets of plate glass (windows of seventeenth century style and size were restored eventually in 1952). He also had an annexe built at the back of the house, which unfortunately obliterated the view and spoiled the garden.

It was here that the young Brunel, coached earnestly by his father who personally educated the child up till the age of nine, not surprisingly began to show an aptitude for things mathematical, mastering the propositions of Euclid at the alarmingly early age of six. Later, at school in Hove, the practical value of his knowledge was used to the detriment of his friends, with whom he

98 Cheyne Walk, where I.K. Brunel spent his childhood

A photograph of Brunel taken at Millwall in 1857. *(National Portrait Gallery)*

once made a bet that a building being erected opposite the school would collapse. It did, the following night. At the age of fourteen, Brunel was sent to France, to Caen and then Paris to study under the great engineer Breguet, returning to the house in Chelsea for holidays. He seems to have been a happy, outgoing child, reported by neighbours to have been always a ringleader at parties, in contrast to his more sedate two sisters, who were apparently 'models of everything young ladies should be'. The novelist Anne Manning, who lived next door, reported that 'there was always something intellectual going on in their home', but Isambard and his friends seem to have found time for more carefree pursuits, such as swimming in the Thames at the foot of the steps in front of the house.

Cheyne Walk was at the time very different from the busy road it is today. As the name implies, it was just a trackway, peaceful and narrow, and journeys into the City were still, in Brunel's time, often made by boat rather than carriage. Many artists and writers came to live along this quiet, attractive waterfront during the nineteenth century.

However, life for Marc Brunel and his family was not all serenity; in 1821 one of his sawmills burnt down and he was sent to King's Bench Prison for debt. He was quickly released, when the Duke of Wellington managed to persuade the authorities to grant Brunel £5000 to discharge himself, on the grounds that he was an asset to the nation. But Marc Brunel was never again a rich man, and his son complained in 1825 while in his father's employ: 'I am most terribly pinched for money . . . we keep neither carriage, nor horse, nor footman, only two maidservants.'

Brunel the engineer

Though I.K. Brunel's engineering projects were to have their impact all over England as well as on other continents (he advised on the building of the Victoria Line railway in Australia and on the Eastern Bengal Railway in India), he had strong associations with London outside the house in which he grew up. It was Brunel who linked London with the West Country by building the Great Western Railway. His initial plan was for the line to cross London, to a terminus at Vauxhall which Brunel saw as the first part of a future link with the continent. However, objectors protested that a railway across London would ruin the air of some of its most exclusive residential areas and so the Great Western terminus was built instead at Paddington.

One of his great achievements in London, a project initiated by Marc Brunel but largely carried out by Isambard, was the boring of the first tunnel under the Thames, between St Mary's, Rotherhithe, and Wapping. It was this work that necessitated the family's removal from Lindsey Row to Bridge Street, Blackfriars, so as to be nearer the construction site.

The making of the tunnel was a long, arduous business, beset with problems. Begun in 1825, it took eighteen years and twenty-three days to complete, *The Times* eventually giving it the predictable nickname of 'The Great Bore'. In spite of this the tunnel never ceased to fascinate Londoners — at one point about seven hundred visitors a day were being attracted to the site to witness the triumphs and inevitable disasters. Finally completed in 1843, the Thames Tunnel is now just another section of the London Underground, between Shoreditch and New Cross.

The building of the Great Eastern at Millwall, 1857. *(St Martin's Prints)*

The 'Great Eastern'

Further up the river still, at Westferry Road, Tower Hamlets, is the spot where Brunel's last and most ambitious work was undertaken. This was the building of the *Great Eastern*, the third of Brunel's great steamships designed to brave the Atlantic. (A commemorative plaque marking the site has recently been removed during demolition work.) The largest steamship of the century (693 feet long), the Great Eastern had to be built broadside on the river. Although again plagued with difficulties, Brunel refused to abandon the project, and the ship, when she was launched in 1858, proved to be stronger and more efficient than the sceptics ever imagined. However, the strain took its toll on Brunel and he died a year later, on 15 September 1859.

Fanny Burney (1752–1840)

11 Bolton Street, W1

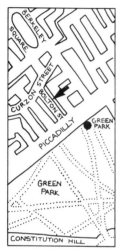

Tube: Green Park.
Bus: Nos. 9, 14, 19, 22, 25, 38.

The Burneys' house in St Martin's Street, which had earlier belonged to Sir Isaac Newton

When Fanny Burney, or Madame D'Arblay as she then was, moved to Bolton Street in 1818, she was an old woman of sixty-six, with a highly eventful life behind her.

Evelina

She had been a young girl of twenty-five when her first novel *Evelina, or The History of a Young Lady's Entrance Into the World*, which took the literary world by storm, was published under an assumed name in January 1778. It was then unheard of for a young lady to write a novel; when she was only fifteen Fanny had written one, but her stepmother, on finding it, had burned it in disgust. So Fanny had written *Evelina* in secret, hidden away in the playroom at the top of the family's large house in St Martin's Street, Leicester Square (demolished in 1925). This house, which had once belonged to Newton (the family watched the Gordon Riots from Newton's observatory on the roof) was frequently the centre of literary and musical gatherings; here Fanny was amused to observe Dr Johnson, on his first visit to the house, poring over the books in the library, 'almost touching the backs of them with his eye-lashes, as he read their titles'.

When Fanny's father, an eminent musician, discovered that his daughter was the authoress of the book he so admired, far from being shocked he delightedly introduced her to his circle, and Fanny was soon lionized by literary London. She became a close friend of Mrs Hester Thrale, and paid frequent visits to the Thrales' house in Streatham, where she first met the ageing Dr Johnson. Fanny was at first stunned by his physical peculiarities: 'His whole great person looked often as if it were going to roll itself, quite voluntarily, from his chair to the floor.' But she quickly learned that he had 'more fun, and comical humour, and love of nonsense about him, than almost anybody', and the two became firm friends.

At Court

But Fanny's life was not entirely happy. She was constantly at odds with her stepmother; and the deaths of her friends Mr

11 Bolton Street, Madame
D'Arblay's home from
1818-28

Thrale in 1781, her mentor Samuel Crisp in 1783, and Johnson in
1784, and perhaps a disappointed romance, led her to accept a
position at Court, and retire almost totally from her family and
social world in 1786. She was looked on with great affection by
the Queen and princesses for her tact and sympathy during
George III's illness in 1788–89. But, though she achieved the
social heights, her letters at the time indicate that she missed her
sisters sorely; eventually her father was persuaded to request her
resignation, and she left the Court in July 1791.

It was on a visit to her sister Susan at Mickleham in Surrey that
Fanny met Alexandre D'Arblay, her future husband, a French
Constitutionalist who had sought refuge at Juniper Hall nearby.
Though her father objected to the emigré's circumstances, the

couple were married in July 1793, and never, according to Fanny, was 'union more blest'. They bought a cottage in Great Bookham, and later built their own house, Camilla Cottage, in West Humble. Fanny had a son in December 1794.

From 1802 the couple lived in France, M. D'Arblay being keen to return to Paris after the war had ended. On Napoleon's return, however, Fanny and M. D'Arblay were forced to flee with other royalists to Brussels, and they eventually settled at Bath in 1815, where Alexandre D'Arblay died in May 1818. Stricken with grief, Fanny decided to move to London so as to be nearer to her son who was at Cambridge, and it was at that point that she took the house in Bolton Street.

Old age

Bolton Street was clean and quiet (it is now rather dull and narrow), chosen for its closeness to Green Park, Hyde Park and St James's, where Madame D'Arblay enjoyed walking, and to Buckingham Gate, where her brother James lived with his family. During the winter of 1818 she was often to be seen walking through the parks, dressed in widow's black. She found London quite lonely, and wrote 'evening society in London is very difficult to be obtained'; and her evenings were chiefly occupied with writing up her experiences, as she had promised her husband she would do, a memoir of her husband's death, and the *Memoirs of Doctor Burney*, published in 1832. She lived in quiet retirement, though old friends like Wilberforce and Walter Scott visited her from time to time — the latter wrote: 'She was an elderly lady, with no remains of personal beauty, but with a single and gentle manner, and pleasing expression of countenance.'

Though she referred in letters to the prospect of ending her days at Bolton Street, Madame D'Arblay in fact lived on until 1840; in 1828 she was persuaded by her son Alex to move to 1 Half Moon Street, Berkeley Square, where he could have a large and well-lit study. The deaths of those who had been close to her were hard to bear; however, she took pleasure in her son's career, and in her many great nieces and nephews, who found her wise, imaginative, and possessed of an extraordinary memory. 'She tells such amusing stories' wrote one '. . . sometimes repeats poetry — takes off all the curious people she used to know, & c. — that you can easily imagine how pleasant it is.' She was touchingly engrossed in her son: 'Alex makes Grandmama as angry as possible with him every night, by bringing home some new book he has bought in the day, while none of her persuasions can induce him to buy a new coat.' When he died in 1837, closely followed by her sister Charlotte (1838) she never really recovered, and died on 6 January 1840; she was buried with her son in Wolcot churchyard, Bath.

Antonio Canaletto (1697–1768)

41 Beak Street, W1

By the time Canaletto came to London in 1746, when he was
nearly fifty, he was already a well-established and popular
painter in his native Venice; his famous canal and river views had
been eagerly purchased by visitors, particularly the British. As
early as 1722, he had received a commission from an Englishman,
and by 1746 the English were his chief patrons. He was well
known to the English through Joseph Smith, later British Consul
in Venice, who acted as a middleman, and Owen McSwiney, who
bought for the Duke of Richmond. Although Horace Walpole
wrote that Smith engaged Canaletto 'to work for him for many
years at a very low price and sold his works to the English at much
higher rates', Canaletto clearly profited as a result of Smith's
sharp eye for the market. No less than fifty of his works, now at
Windsor, were acquired through Smith by George III.

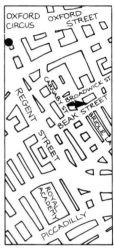

Tube: Oxford Circus or
Piccadilly Circus.
Bus: Nos. 3, 6, 12, 13, 15,
53, 88, 159.

London beckons

It was not surprising, therefore, that in 1746 Canaletto decided
to go to London himself, since the Austrian War of Succession
had begun to have an adverse effect on the flow into Europe of
British aristocrats who would spend money on the arts. He
brought with him glowing letters of introduction and a commission
by the Duke of Richmond to paint a view of the Thames from his
dining room.

Canaletto took rooms in Silver Street (now Beak Street), which
ran to the north of Golden Square, in the house of Mr Richard
Wiggan, a cabinet maker. It was not a particularly desirable
neighbourhood. Development of the area had begun in the
seventeenth century, and the buildings had been laid out with
little regard for a coherent street pattern — a fact which is still
evident today. Regent Street with its grand buildings did not
then exist, and in its place lay Swallow Street, 'long, ugly and
irregular', while Silver Street was then described as a 'narrow
back street, incommodiously situated'. It was an area of four-
storey houses intended for tradesmen and their tenants, whereas
Golden Square, designed for the gentry and completed by the
early 1700s, was more fashionable. Only later, when West London
became fashionable, did the gentry move out, and the area

41 Beak Street

became popular with foreign residents.

No. 41 has been altered since Canaletto lived there — inside there is little evidence of the period — but the brick façade, though altered by the shop front and the modification of the upper floor windows, is still characteristic of the latter half of the eighteenth century. We know that Canaletto worked in a studio with a skylight situated in the garden at the back of the house. It was to this studio that Canaletto on at least two occasions invited an audience to watch him paint. It seems that other artists, jealous of his success, were spreading rumours that he was not the real Canaletto but an imitator: so he announced in the press that:

> Signor Canaletto hereby invites any Gentleman that will
> be pleased to come to his house, to see a Picture done by
> him, being A View of St James's Park, which he hopes
> may in some Measure deserve their Approbation.

Success

Canaletto stayed in London, in this house, almost continuously until 1755, his works constantly popular. The first two views of London (now at Goodwood House) which he painted from Richmond House were particularly fine — perhaps two of the

best views of London ever painted. He painted a number of views, not only of London but of castles, country houses and rivers, with such success that he was still painting English scenes after his return to Venice. His realistic, lucid, and firm manner of painting suited the demands of clients for accurate views of London which were nonetheless flattering; his commercial success was assured, though arguably he never he surpassed his first two English works, perhaps as the memory of Venetian sunshine faded under London's grey skies. But the Thames, his most popular subject, was a constant inspiration. Even though by this time the great buildings which had once lined the Thames had disappeared, it was still both a beautiful scene and a busy highway, giving him the opportunity to paint the bustling river traffic, as well as the construction of the new Westminster Bridge. When he left England he had firmly established a vogue for views of London, and many imitators eagerly filled the vacuum created by his departure.

View of the City and St Paul's Cathedral from the terrace of Somerset House (detail), by Canaletto. (Reproduced by gracious permission of Her Majesty The Queen)

Thomas Carlyle (1795–1881)

24 Cheyne Row, SW3

Tube: South Kensington.
Bus: Nos. 11, 19, 22, 39, 45, 49.

In 1887, six years after Carlyle's death, Oliver Wendell Holmes went to Chelsea in search of Carlyle's former home, 24 Cheyne Row. He found it 'a dingy three-storey brick house, far from attractive. It was untenanted, neglected, its windows were unwashed, a pane of glass broken, its threshold appeared untrodden, its whole aspect forlorn and desolate.' Much has changed since then: Carlyle's house is now a museum, and perhaps the most eloquent literary shrine in London.

Cheap and excellent

It was in 1834, when Carlyle first decided to settle permanently in London, that he looked over a house in Cheyne Row. He had hunted high and low, from Hampstead to Kensington, for a suitable house for himself and his wife Jane, still at home in Craigenputtock in the Scottish Lowlands. Eventually, on a visit to Leigh Hunt (who lived in Upper Cheyne Row, Chelsea), he had a stroke of luck. He wrote excitedly to Jane:

> Not a gunshot from Hunt's I came upon another house, greatly the best in quality and quantity I have yet seen . . . . Chelsea is unfashionable; it was once the resort of the Court and great, however; hence numerous old houses, at once cheap and excellent.

One would hardly describe this part of Chelsea now, with its air of self-conscious gentility, as unfashionable! However, the village at that time appears to have had advantages perhaps less apparent to today's residents: 'Chelsea abounds more than any other place in omnibi, and they take you to Coventry Street for sixpence.' Cheyne Row lies close to the Thames, just off Cheyne Walk, and consisted then of a terrace of eleven houses, built in 1708. Ten of these, now nos. 16–34, remain, of which no. 24 (then no. 5), the house looked at by Carlyle, was fairly typical, faced in red and brown brick. The site of what was the eleventh house of the Row, at the northern end, is now occupied by a Roman Catholic Church.

Carlyle continued his letter:

Carlyle in the garden at 24
Cheyne Row, 1857.
(National Trust)

The House itself is eminent, antique; wainscotted to the
very ceiling, and has been all new-painted and repaired;
broadish stair, with massive balustrade (in the old style)
corniced and as thick as one's thigh; floors firm as a rock,
wood of them here and there worm-eaten yet capable of
cleanness, and still thrice the strength of a modern floor.
And then as to room, Goody! . . . Three storeys beside
the sunk storey; in every one of them *three* apartments in
depth (something like forty feet in all; for it was thirteen
of my steps!)

His wife replied cautiously:

I have great liking to that massive old concern . . . But is
it not too near the river? I should fear it would be a very
foggy situation in the winter, and always damp and
unwholesome. And the wainscot up to the ceilings . . . if
bugs have been in the house! Must they not have found
there as well as the inmates 'room without end'?

Shortly afterwards, Jane Carlyle joined her husband in London
at the lodgings in 33 Ampton Street (now marked by a blue
plaque) where he had been staying for the previous month, and
where they had both spent the winter of 1831–32. Together they
decided that the Chelsea house was 'nearly twice as good as any
other we could get for the money' and finally took possession of
no. 5 Cheyne Row on 10 June 1834. The rent was just £35, and
remained the same throughout the forty-seven years of the
Carlyles' residence.

24 Cheyne Row. The house, now run by the National Trust, is open to the public from April-October, Wed-Sat 11.00-17.00 and Sun 14.00-17.00. (Tel. 01-352 7087)

Powerful personality

The Carlyles remained here for the rest of their lives: Jane died in 1866, and Thomas lived on until 1881. Here Carlyle wrote his three greatest works, *The French Revolution* (1837), *Life and Letters of Oliver Cromwell* (1845) and *Frederick the Great* (1851–65) which together established him as the most respected historian of his time. Indeed, soon after his arrival in London his powerful personality had made him something of a curiosity in the literary world, and the house at Ampton Street attracted many of the distinguished *literati* of the day, who followed him to the modest house in Chelsea. It was here that a distraught John Stuart Mill had to inform Carlyle, who had lent Mill his only manuscript of the first volume of *The French Revolution*, that his maid had used it as a firelighter. Having destroyed his notes, Carlyle had to rewrite the whole work from scratch.

Though for a while after Carlyle's death his house in Cheyne Row stood untenanted and fell into the condition in which Wendell Holmes found it, this state of affairs did not persist for long. So great was the veneration in which Carlyle was held by the Victorians that in 1895 the house was purchased by public subscription, and the Carlyle House Memorial Trust set up to restore and administer the property. In July 1896 the house was first opened to the public, and Carlyle's House has remained open ever since. The guide book now in use is substantially that written by Carlyle's nephew Alexander, for the museum's very earliest visitors.

Memorial

The house today is strongly evocative of the Carlyles' presence, perhaps not only because they resided here so long but because the house was made a memorial at such an early date, before subsequent tenants could make alterations. As a result, the furnishings and decorations are almost exactly as they were in the Carlyles' time: though the carpets have been replaced, some furniture and other items added, and some of the panelling removed, the latter still reminds one of Carlyle's first impression, of a house 'wainscotted to the very ceiling'. The sitting-room or parlour, described by Carlyle as 'in the highest degree comfortable and serviceable', looks almost exactly as it did when Robert Tait painted *A Chelsea Interior (The Carlyles at Home)* which now hangs in the room.

The visitor's tour of the house ends in the attic room which Carlyle had built at the top of the house. He was so irritated by the noises of the neighbourhood — cocks crowing, pianos playing and passing river traffic — that he decided to have this new room built specially soundproofed, with double walls, a skylight and no windows, to be his study. Carlyle used the study for twelve years while writing *Frederick the Great*, but the room in fact turned out to be the noisiest in the house, somehow magnifying the sounds from the river! Resignedly, Carlyle finally withdrew to the ground floor; the room was made a bedroom, but has been refurnished as the study, and photographs taken in 1857 reveal how little it has altered since then.

Charlie Chaplin (1889–1977)

287 Kennington Road, SE11

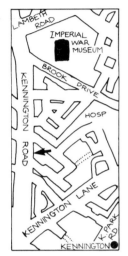

Tube: Kennington.
Bus: Nos. 3, 109, 155, 159, 172.

The phrase 'rags to riches' could hardly be applied more appropriately to anyone than to Charlie Chaplin. From a destitute childhood in Lambeth, he became perhaps the greatest comic actor of the century.

A plaque now adorns a sombre Victorian terraced house in Kennington Road in Lambeth where two rooms on the first floor were once home for Charlie Chaplin. It was one of many tenements on or near the Kennington Road where he lived as a child until he escaped from the acute destitution of the area, determined to become an actor. As he wrote in his autobiography, until the opening of Westminster Bridge in 1750, the Kennington Road had been merely a bridle path; but then a new road was built from London to Brighton, and as a result the Kennington Road

> boasted some fine houses of architectural merit, fronted with iron grill balconies from which occupants could once have seen George IV coaching on his way to Brighton.

But by 1889, the year he was born, most of the houses were in various stages of deterioration, and had become rooming houses or apartments.

Workhouse

In his early years, however, things were not so bad. Charlie's parents were both vaudeville players, separated when he was a year old, but he and his brother Sydney lived with their mother in relative luxury in 'three tastefully furnished rooms' in West Square, St George's Road, Lambeth. But then a crisis occurred: Charlie's mother had lost her singing voice permanently through illness, and when her husband stopped paying alimony there was no alternative but for her to enter the Lambeth workhouse, while Charlie and Sydney attended the Hanwell School for Orphans and Destitute Children. Soon after, they heard that their mother had been sent to a lunatic asylum; and seven-year-old Charlie and his elder brother found themselves being driven in a bread van to 287 Kennington Road, where their father lived with a lady named Louise and their small son.

The months spent here were perhaps the most dismal part of

Opposite: 287 Kennington Road, where the Chaplin family lived on the first floor

Charlie's childhood. He wrote in *My Autobiography*:

> The family lived in two rooms and, although the front
> room had large windows, the light filtered in as if from
> under water. Everything looked as sad as Louise; the
> wallpaper looked sad, the horse-hair furniture looked
> sad, and the stuffed pike in a glass case that had
> swallowed another pike as large as itself — the head
> sticking out of its mouth — looked gruesomely sad.

Charlie and Sydney were sent to Kennington Road School, which
offered some escape from Louise, who would constantly taunt
Sydney, to whom she had taken a violent dislike:

> Sometimes on a Saturday night, feeling deeply
> despondent, I would hear the lively music of a concertina
> passing by the back bedroom window, playing a highland
> march, accompanied by rowdy youths and giggling coster
> girls. The vigour and vitality of it seemed ruthlessly
> indifferent to my unhappiness.

Child actor

Finally, Mother came back. The boys gratefully left 287 Kennington Road, and the family vacillated from room to room,
finally settling for a while in a tiny garret at 3 Pownall Terrace, a
derelict row of houses (destroyed in the Blitz) set back from the
Kennington Road. Charlie had now persuaded his mother to let
him leave school, and he had a variety of short-lived professions
— newsvendor, printer, toymaker, and glassblower — but money
was still desperately short. But life was soon to alter drastically:
Charlie had never lost sight of his dream, instilled by his mother
at an early age, of becoming an actor, and, at the age of nine, he
toured the country with a troop of clog dancers —Mr Jackson's
Eight Lancashire Lads. It was a humble beginning: but at twelve,
when his mother was again taken to an asylum, he and Sydney
were determined to get on the stage, and Charlie was given a star
part in *Jim, The Romance of a Cockney* at the Kingston Theatre.
The play was a flop, but Charlie was singled out by the critics for
special praise:

> Although hackneyed and old-fashioned, Sammy was
> made vastly amusing by Master Charles Chaplin, a
> bright and vigorous child actor. I have never heard of the
> boy before, but I hope to hear great things of him in the
> near future.

The critic was not disappointed: it was the first of many successes
that were to take Charlie to Hollywood, far away from the poverty
of the Kennington Road.

Sir Winston Churchill (1874–1965)

28 Hyde Park Gate, SW7

The 1945 General Election suddenly and unexpectedly saw Winston Churchill out of office. It left him without a London home, as of course he now had to leave Downing Street; and although he spent much of his time at Chartwell, the country house in Kent which he had bought in 1922, he still needed a London base. He quickly found and purchased 28 Hyde Park Gate, a charming town house in a quiet *cul-de-sac*. It was to remain his London home until his death, apart from the period when he was again in office from 1951–55, during which time it was let to the Spanish Ambassador.

Revenge

Despite the shock of severe defeat, at a time when Churchill was already over seventy, there was no question of him not becoming Leader of the Opposition. Although he spent much of 1946 touring the United States (where he made his famous 'Iron Curtain' speech which caused a furore at the time) and Western Europe, he was still active in the Commons, and campaigned in the election battles of 1950 and 1951. He was determined to get his revenge on the Labour government:

> A short while ago I was ready to retire and die gracefully.
> Now I'm going to stay and have them out.

He was also able to return to writing, which he had abandoned during the War, and from 1948 the volumes of his *Second World War* appeared at roughly annual intervals. Life alternated between Chartwell and Hyde Park Gate: it soon became clear that the latter house, while an ideal *pied-à-terre*, was not large enough to entertain all those who wished to see him, but fortunately the house next door, no. 27, came on the market, and Churchill was able to purchase it and have nos. 27 and 28 turned into a single, much bigger, house in which he could entertain and also accommodate his large staff.

After resigning from the Premiership in April 1955, he again turned to writing: he had already prepared some of the *History of the English-speaking Peoples*, but now had to revise the parts he had written before the War. The four volumes came out between

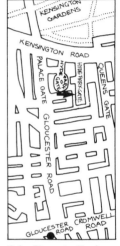

Tube: Gloucester Road.
Bus: Nos. 9, 33, 49, 52, 73.

28 Hyde Park Gate,
purchased by Churchill in
1945

1956 and 1958, receiving rather a cautious welcome from historians. He remained an active MP, declining a peerage so that he could remain in the Commons, though in later years a number of small strokes and increasing deafness made his attendance more difficult, and he eventually retired in 1964.

Inevitably, Churchill was greatly saddened at the deaths of many of his close friends, and although he celebrated his ninetieth birthday in style at Hyde Park Gate, relishing the occasion and appearing at a window to greet the crowds who had gathered outside, there was little to keep him going. On 15 January 1965 he had another stroke: daily bulletins were read to the journalists and photographers who gathered outside Hyde Park Gate, informing them of the state of his health, until his death nine days later. He was accorded the honour of a state funeral, and was buried at Bladon, near Blenheim Palace, the home of his ancestors.

Robert, Lord Clive (1725–74)

45 Berkeley Square, W1

Robert Clive was born on 29 September 1725 at Styche, the family home near Market Drayton in Shropshire. Forty-nine years later he committed suicide at his London home, 45 Berkeley Square. In this comparatively short lifetime, he had become one of the most famous figures in English history.

At school in Market Drayton, Clive seems to have shown many of the characteristics as a child that would today have labelled him a juvenile delinquent. His uncle Daniel Bayley, in whose house, Hope Hall in Manchester, Robert spent some of his childhood, wrote of Robert that he was 'out of measure addicted to fighting'. Apparently he obtained 'protection money' from shopkeepers in the village to guarantee them freedom from his and his schoolfriends' window-breaking.

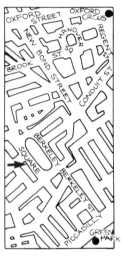

Tube: Bond Street and Green Park.
Bus: No. 25.

From Market Drayton Robert went briefly to Merchant Taylors school in London, with little evident profit, and later to a private school in Hemel Hempstead, whence he left at the age of eighteen for Madras in India as a clerk in the East India Company, arriving late in 1744. Office life made him moody and quarrelsome — apparently he twice tried to commit suicide — and it was not long before he took up a military career. He made rapid progress: he was instrumental in the turnabout of fortunes which led, by 1752, to complete British control of India at the expense of the French, and by 1753 when he returned to England and stayed in London for the first time, he was a rich and famous man.

However, he dissipated his money at an alarming rate, and in 1755 was forced to return to India; by the time he came back to London in 1760 he was again rich, and had achieved international fame for his victory at Plassey. Recognition was heaped upon him: in 1764 he was knighted, and he became MP for Shrewsbury.

Oriental magnificence

While in London, Clive and his wife stayed for a time at Swithins Lane (an address also used by his father) until, in the autumn of 1761, he purchased no. 45 Berkeley Square on a ninety-year lease from the Earl of Ancram. His biographer Gleig tells us that it was a splendid and spacious house, 'fitted up in a style of oriental magnificence' by Clive. In the second half of the eighteenth

century Berkeley Square was at the height of its elegance; developed in the late seventeenth century, unlike many squares at the time it was not built to a single design, which lent it a particular character and charm. Though many houses in the Square have since been spoiled, no. 45 and its neighbour 46 are still very fine houses; an extra storey was added to no. 45 in 1830, but otherwise it remains little altered, the first-floor windows having fine eighteenth-century pediments and balcony balustrades. Inside, the spacious entrance hall is connected by Ionic columns with an imposing staircase.

Opposite: 45 Berkeley Square, where Clive committed suicide

Perhaps inevitably, Clive's phenomenal success had made him many enemies. His second governorship of Bengal from May 1765 to the end of 1766 was perhaps his crowning achievement, a triumph of statesmanship; but although he rectified many of the errors of his previous administrations, he had made enemies in the civil service and army by his repression of corruption and abuse. They and many others formed a cabal against him, and the press had a field day accusing him of corrupt dealings and of accepting huge bribes in the form of gifts whilst he was in India. In 1772 a parliamentary committee uncovered evidence of corruption amongst East India Company employees which seemed to implicate Clive. But he defended himself brilliantly in Parliament against the allegations, and in May 1773 when his name was cleared it was resolved that he had 'rendered great and meritorious services to his country'.

Suicide

However, the strain undoubtedly took its toll upon Clive's melancholic temperament. It seems that he had long been using opium to relieve a painful internal disorder, and though the evidence is only circumstantial, it seems very likely that on 22 November 1774, at his house in Berkeley Square, he knowingly took his own life. According to Horace Walpole, Clive's doctor 'gave him one dose of laudanum, but he wanted another, upon which the doctor said that a second dose would result in death. Even so he took it, and with fatal effects.' But rumours were rife, and the next day Walpole wrote that 'at present it is most fashionable to believe he cut his throat'. The distress felt by his wife is evident in a touching anecdote told by Lady Mary Coke. She recalled that when Lady Clive discovered the body

> weltering in his blood, 'tis no wonder the horrour of the scene should have such an effect upon her spirits as to deprive her of her senses, and throw her with a fit, but 'tis fortunate. She remained in it so long, that when she came out of it, her ideas were so confused with regard to that terrible scene, that She believed to have been a dream what was but too real ... She was incouraged in this notion, and was told he was dead of an apoplectick fit.

John Constable (1776–1837)

40 Well Walk, NW3

Tube: Hampstead.
Bus: Nos. 24, 46, 187, 268, C11.

When Constable first moved to Hampstead in 1821, the village did not yet have the artistic image it was later to acquire; indeed, Constable was one of the first artists of any renown to live there, and only later did a large artistic colony develop. It was at the time a highly respectable village, and particularly popular as a place of residence with 'professionals' from the City and West End; an excellent transport service of regular short-stage carriages had developed, making commuting an easy, if expensive, business. Constable himself was one of these early commuters, since he continued to work in his studio in Soho.

Marriage

Constable had moved to London from his native East Bergholt in Suffolk in 1795, when he had been accepted, at the age of nineteen, as a student at the Royal Academy schools. He lived in a variety of lodgings, living for a while in Charlotte Street, Soho, and then moving to Keppel Street in Bloomsbury. When he married his long-standing sweetheart Maria Bicknell in 1817, the house in Keppel Street after a while proved rather small for their growing family, and Constable found new lodgings in 1822 at no. 76 Charlotte Street. (This house, once marked by a plaque, has since been demolished, and an office block stands on the site.) Many repairs and alterations were necessary when they first moved in, but the house, which Constable retained until his death, was finally in order, and he wrote: 'I have got the large painting room into excellent order; it is light, airy, sweet and warm.'

However, his wife's constant ill-health and the illness of his eldest son caused Constable to search for a new home in the country, and after wandering from place to place the family finally settled in Hampstead. They were first living in Hampstead as early as 1821 at 2 Lower Terrace, and then moved to a house in Downshire Hill, before finally settling at no. 40 (then no. 6) Well Walk. The name of the street recalled the heady days of the late seventeenth century when Hampstead enjoyed a brief period of popularity as a fashionable spa because of its chalybeate springs, when it had acquired a pump room, assembly room and ballroom.

40 Well Walk – a
'comfortable little house'

(A privately erected plaque at Wellside, Well Walk, commemorates
the site of the pump room.)

The Constables were extremely fond of the house. In August
1827 Constable wrote to a friend:

> We are at length fixed in our comfortable little house in
> Well Walk, Hampstead and are once more enjoying our
> own furniture, and sleeping in our own beds. My plans in
> search of health for my family have been ruinous; but I
> hope now that our movable camp no longer exists, and
> that I am settled for life .... The house is to my wife's
> content.

They aimed now to make Hampstead their permanent place of
residence, retaining part of the house in Charlotte Street as
Constable's studio and letting out the rest to bring in some much
needed cash. Their seventh child was born in Hampstead in
January 1828.

New inspiration

Though Suffolk continued to provide much of the inspiration for
his work, Constable the artist delighted in Hampstead, spending
much of his time wandering on the Heath observing the changing
patterns of the sky. He wrote enthusiastically of the view from
their house:

> Our little drawing-room commands a view unsurpassed
> in Europe, from Westminster Abbey to Gravesend. The

76 Charlotte Street (since demolished), the house in Soho where Constable died

dome of St Paul's in the air seems to realize Michael Angelo's words on seeing the Pantheon: 'I will build such a thing in the sky.'

The watercolour views of London which he produced echo the spirit of his words. Several other of his paintings of Hampstead survive, showing that he also loved to sketch in oils the famous Hampstead Ponds which derived from the natural springs (Branch Mill Pond, which inspired several such sketches, still remains). Other works done by Constable while at Hampstead include the famous *Dedham Vale*, which he diffidently described as 'a large upright landscape, perhaps my best'.

Constable's hope that his wife's health would improve with the move to Hampstead sadly proved to be in vain. Her slow death from consumption was extremely painful to him, as Constable's friend Leslie recorded after one visit to the house:

I was at Hampstead a few days before she breathed her last. She was then on a sofa in their cheerful parlour, and although Constable appeared in his usual spirits in her presence, yet before I left the house he took me into another room, wrung my hand, and burst into tears, without speaking.

After her death, in 1828, Constable continued to spend much of his time in Hampstead. The death of Maria's father shortly before had brought some financial security to the long impecunious family, so Constable was able both to employ a housekeeper to look after the children and to keep on the Hampstead house.

Ironically, the personal sorrow of his wife's death was swiftly followed by professional recognition: in 1829 Constable was at last made a full Royal Academician, an honour long denied to him, as his style of landscape painting, which was neither melodramatic nor overtly picturesque, did not accord with contemporary taste. Though he was more successful in selling his Hampstead sketches than any others, it is strange to think that when the National Gallery was first set up in 1828, only one of Constable's paintings, *The Cornfield*, was chosen for inclusion.

Much of the latter part of Constable's tenancy of 40 Well Walk was taken up with the preparation of the prints for his *English Landscape*, a collection of mezzotints of his work, and which consumed much of his time and energy. He seems to have retained the house in Hampstead at least until 1834, and died in his little attic bedroom in Charlotte Street from an attack of indigestion on 31 March 1837. (There is a monument to Constable in St John's churchyard, Hampstead.)

Noel Coward (1899–1973)

17 Gerald Road, SW1

In contrast to what one might expect, Noel Coward was brought up not with a silver spoon in his mouth but in genteel poverty in south London: starting life in an 'unpretentious abode' as he described 'Helmsdale', Waldegrave Road, Teddington, Middlesex, the family moved thence to Sutton, Battersea and Clapham Common. Finally they moved, in 1917, to the address where Noel became famous, 111 Ebury Street, SW1 — the street where Mozart (whose music Noel never liked) had stayed as a child.

Noel's Aunt Ida had successfully run a guesthouse in the street for many years, and when the lease of a house opposite went up for sale, Mrs Coward, determined to end the years of poverty caused chiefly by her husband's innate idleness, decided to take it on. Noel, happy to be nearer the West End where he was already on the stage (he had made his first professional appearance at the age of ten), had a tiny attic room at the top of the guesthouse, where Mrs Coward nobly struggled with her sons' help to take care of 'The Lodgers'.

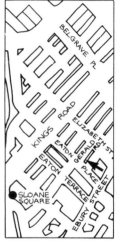

Tube: Sloane Square or Victoria.
Bus: Nos. 10, 11, 16, 25, 38, 39, 52, 137, 149, 500, 503, 507.

Astonishing promise

Noel seems to have moved down the house at Ebury Street as he made his way, slowly and uncertainly, up in the theatrical world. By the time he was twenty, in 1919, he had appeared in the leading role of one of his own comedies, *I'll Leave It to You*, and was suddenly acclaimed by the critics as a playwright of astonishing promise for one so young. He had made a great many friends, and moved from his little attic to a room of larger proportions on the floor below, where he could entertain in style and display his grand piano in suitable surroundings.

But Noel's first major triumph came in 1924: the production of his play *The Vortex* at the Everyman Theatre, Hampstead. He later wrote:

> *The Vortex* was an immediate success and established me both as a playwright and as an actor, which was fortunate, because until then I had not proved myself to be so hot in either capacity.

Indeed, the play was very nearly called off: less than a week

17 Gerald Road, Noel
Coward's 'studio'

before the opening, the Lord Chamberlain refused to grant the
play a licence, on account of what he considered to be its
risqué content (Noel, in the leading role, played the part of a
young drug addict). However, on the morning of the first night,
Noel visited the Lord Chamberlain, and informed him that, in
fact, the play was a highly moral tract. His Lordship was
persuaded: and the play was a roaring success, transferring
swiftly to the West End. In celebration of his rising fortunes,
Noel yet again moved down the house in Ebury Street, this
time taking over the whole first floor, which he re-decorated,
adorning his bedroom with scarlet walls embellished with
murals. Despite the fact that from now on Noel's successes
were frequently followed by disastrous flops — such as
Sirocco in 1928, when Noel and Ivor Novello were booed off
the stage and spat upon from the gallery — the image of Noel
Coward as a rich and idle dilettante who dashed off his plays
with effortless ease in a few days, however far it was from the
truth, was firmly fixed in the adoring public's mind.

The 'studio'

Despite such setbacks as *Sirocco*, by 1928 Noel was wealthy
enough to enable him to move his family to Gouldenhurst Farm,

on his beloved Romney Marsh. 111 Ebury Street was sold, though Noel continued to rent his suite of rooms there from the new owners, until he moved to 17 Gerald Road nearby two years later. His new 'studio' as he and his friends referred to it, continued to be his London home for many years; now marked by a privately erected plaque, it was the upper part of a large house, lying back from the road and approached by a dense tunnel of trees. The house had previously been leased to an interior designer, whose influence could be detected in the large, light studio and antique fittings. Noel soon established his own style, choosing modern fabrics, zebra-striped cushions and fashionable 1930s *objets d'art*.

It was shortly after moving here in 1930, the year that *Private Lives* opened, that Noel, with an idea in his head for a new and ambitious play but unable to decide on a setting, happened to be browsing in Foyles in Charing Cross Road through some old bound copies of the *Illustrated London News*. Suddenly, coming across a full-page picture of a troopship leaving for the Boer War, inspiration struck; he bought the volumes, and back at Gerald Road happily recalled the great songs of the era. He had found what he wanted, and with the aid of his friend 'Peter' Stern who arrived for tea he hit on the idea and setting for *Cavalcade*, one of the most ambitious plays of the period tracing the history of two families through the first thirty years of the twentieth century. First performed in 1931, the play became, unintended by Noel, a symbol of patriotism, at a time when the nation's security was shaken by the Depression.

Noel was to stay at Gerald Road for many years: the pre-war years which saw his greatest successes; the war years when he worked on the films *In Which We Serve* and *Brief Encounter* at home and entertained troops abroad; the post-war years during which his reputation fell into drastic decline. Finally in 1955, after a series of disastrous performances in America had made it impossible for him to meet the demands of the Inland Revenue, he sadly sold up both Gouldenhurst and 17 Gerald Road to live abroad for good. He wrote sadly of the latter:

It is . . . horrid to feel that I shall never live there again, never have relish in the magic power of walking briskly up the alleyway, bounding up the stairs, leaving a 'To be called' note on the round table and returning to my cosy little bedroom where, let's face it, a *great deal* has happened during the last twenty-six years.

Charles Dickens (1812–70)

48 Doughty Street, WC1

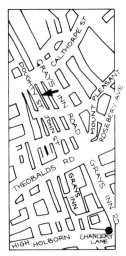

Tube: Chancery Lane.
Bus: Nos. 5, 18, 19, 38, 45, 46, 55, 171, 172, 243, 259.

Dickens moved to 48 Doughty Street in March 1837 from Furnival's Inn, where he had lived with his wife Kate since their marriage in April of the previous year. They brought with them their first son Charles, Kate's younger sister Mary Hogarth, and Dickens' younger brother, Fred. The spacious Doughty Street house, a four-storeyed, late eighteenth century building, provided plenty of room for the Dickens' menage.

The street itself was highly respectable, with gates at either end attended by porters, who were clad in mulberry-coloured livery and wore gold-laced hats. It was all a far cry from Dickens' poverty-stricken childhood. Though his early years had been spent in Chatham, Kent, the Dickens family came to London in 1823, where they lodged briefly in a run-down house in Bayham Street, Camden Town, from whence, after falling in debt, John Dickens, Charles's father, was removed to the Marshalsea prison. For a while, in order to make ends meet, Charles was sent to work in a blacking factory, at the foot of Hungerford steps by the river Thames. Though an inheritance revived the family's fortunes, enabling the young Charles to return to school and afterwards to work for a solicitor, he always remembered with horror the experience of the blacking factory and his family's grim poverty.

Grief

However, the Doughty Street house promised happiness and prosperity, and the serialization of *Pickwick Papers* began a few days after the move. But the household suffered a severe loss only a few weeks later when Mary Hogarth, aged only seventeen, the sister-in-law to whom Dickens was devoted, died suddenly one evening after she, Charles and Kate had returned from the theatre. Dickens was paralysed with grief, and was for a while unable to continue with his work. Mary was thereafter always idealized in his imagination (she is the model for Little Nell), and the fact that Dickens' wife was unable to match the endless charm and goodness of her sister in Dickens' eyes probably contributed to the eventual failure of their marriage.

However, after a while Dickens was able to work again, and the two years spent at Doughty Street were a prolific time for him.

48 Doughty Street, which
now houses a collection
of Dickens memorabilia.
It is open to the public
throughout the year, Mon-
Sat 10.00-17.00.
(Tel. 01-405 2127)

Here he wrote both *Pickwick Papers* and *Oliver Twist* for monthly publication, finishing the former in November 1837 and the latter in the autumn of 1838. On completing *Pickwick*, he was invited by his publishers to write another novel of similar length and style. Soon afterwards he travelled to Yorkshire to study the cheap boarding schools there, and immediately after his return to Doughty Street in February 1838 set to work on *Nicholas Nickleby*, which was published that October. He also started work here on *Barnaby Rudge*, though publication was not begun until after he had left Doughty Street.

Portrait of Dickens by
Daniel Maclise, 1839, the
year he left Doughty Street.
(Tate Gallery)

Social life

The phenomenal success of *Pickwick Papers*, followed by that of *Oliver Twist*, ensured that Dickens' name, already known through his parliamentary reporting and his *Sketches by Boz*, became famous while he was at Doughty Street. Dickens led an almost feverish social life, particularly after the death of Mary; he thus met many of the leading artists and writers of the day, many of whom were visitors to the house. One admirer who came here, Leigh Hunt, voiced the impression of many others when he remarked: 'What a face is his to meet in a drawing-room. It has the life and soul in it of fifty human beings.' Though Dickens was easily distracted from his work by the sound of the bells of St Paul's — he complained 'I can hardly hear my own ideas as they come into my head, and say what they mean' — visitors seem not to have bothered him: his brother-in-law wrote an amusing account of how Dickens was able to sit happily writing *Oliver Twist* while at the same time joining in a chatty conversation with his wife and guests. He would relax by going riding, one of his favourite occupations while at Doughty Street: he once invited his friend and later biographer Forster to 'join him at 11 am in a fifteen-mile ride out and ditto in, lunch on the road, with a six-o'clock dinner at Doughty Street' — a form of exercise which Forster found excessively strenuous.

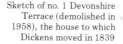

Sketch of no. 1 Devonshire
Terrace (demolished in
1958), the house to which
Dickens moved in 1839

By the end of 1839, Dickens had decided to move: the birth of two daughters, Mamie and Kate, at Doughty Street, made a larger house necessary, apart from the fact that Dickens felt that his present house no longer reflected his success and income adequately. He found a suitable house, of ' "undeniable" situation and excessive splendour' at 1 Devonshire Terrace, near Regent's Park, and moved late in 1839. This house, in which he stayed until 1851, was unfortunately demolished in 1958.

48 Doughty Street is now a Dickens Museum, making a convenient starting point for anyone wishing to delve into the wealth of Dickensian associations in London. Though little of the furniture used by Dickens while he lived there remains, much of that now in the house was owned by him at his last home, Gads Hill Place, Rochester, Kent. The house also has a rich collection of Dickensiana — even the window through which Bill Sykes is said to have pushed Oliver on the occasion of the burglary in *Oliver Twist*.

Benjamin Disraeli (1804–81)

22 Theobalds Road, WC1 and 19 Curzon Street, W1

Just around the corner from Dickens' House in Doughty Street is the birthplace of Benjamin Disraeli, at 22 Theobalds Road, Holborn, formerly known as 6 King's Road. Another plaque in London marks the house in which he died, at 19 Curzon Street, Mayfair.

Though Disraeli himself was never quite sure where he was born and named various different houses as his birthplace, it has now been established beyond reasonable doubt that it was in fact 22 Theobalds Road. This part of Holborn, near Gray's Inn, was then highly fashionable, and the house was plain but imposing, with four storeys and a basement, a conventional late Georgian terrace. The terraced row, nos. 14–22, has been very well preserved, and both the exterior and interior of no. 22 contain features of great architectural merit, including the original doorcase.

Benjamin's father, Isaac D'Israeli, a novelist, wrote several books in the house. From here Benjamin went to school in Islington, and his father noted one trait in the child which hardly indicated what his future choice of career was to be: 'He never lies.' The D'Israelis left Theobalds Road in 1818, and moved to 6 Bloomsbury Square, enabling Isaac to be near his favourite haunt, the British Museum. Later, in 1826, he took a country estate, Bradenham Manor, at the foot of the Chilterns.

Theobalds Road:
Tube: Chancery Lane or Holborn.
Bus: Nos. 5, 18, 19, 38, 45, 46, 55, 171, 172, 243, 259.

Career

On leaving school at the age of seventeen, Benjamin Disraeli spent three years as an articled clerk to a solicitor, before deciding to seek his fortune gambling on the stock market, a venture which landed him heavily in debt. Turning to journalism, he subsequently wrote a romantic novel, *Vivian Grey*, which was published in 1826 and met with commerical success if not literary acclaim. Further writing brought him a reasonable income.

On his return from a tour of Europe and the Middle East in 1832 Disraeli decided to go into politics — fortunately for him his father had severed his connection with the Jewish faith in 1813 and had his children baptised, since Jews were not then eligible for Parliament. Disraeli finally entered Parliament as Conservative

22 Theobalds Road, where
Disraeli was born

MP for Maidstone, Kent in 1837, after standing unsuccessfully no less than four times.

Disraeli rapidly gained stature in Parliament after a disastrous maiden speech which led him to declare: 'I sit down now, but the time will come when you *will* hear me.' He soon gained a reputation as one of the Commons' greatest orators, and in 1848 was made leader of the Conservative party in the House of Commons. In 1852, 1858–59 and 1866–67 he served as Chancellor of the Exchequer, and finally became Prime Minister in 1868 and again from 1874–80, being made Earl of Beaconsfield in 1876.

After residing briefly at a number of London addresses,

Disraeli had married in 1839 a wealthy widow, Mrs Wyndham Lewis, and moved into her house at 1 Grosvenor Gate (now 29 Park Lane). This was his residence for many years, where he wrote *Sybil* and *Coningsby*, and like 22 Theobalds Road and 19 Curzon Street the house still survives, an unusually high tally of surviving London residences. In 1848, having become MP for Buckinghamshire, he purchased, in addition to his London home, a delightful country estate, Hughenden Manor, situated in the Chilterns near High Wycombe. The estate, still intact, remained in the family until comparatively recently and the house, quite small by the standards of the day but well situated overlooking a picturesque valley, is now a Disraeli museum.

19 Curzon Street, Disraeli's last London home

Fallen statesman

It was not until late in life that Disraeli moved to no. 19 Curzon Street. After the Conservative Government had been soundly defeated in the general election of 1880, putting Disraeli out of Downing Street, he had no London residence. For the time being, when in London, he had to stay with friends, such as Lord and Lady Salisbury and the Rothschilds. But he wanted a London home — 'I always wanted to die in London,' he wrote, conscious of his age —'it gives one six months more of life, and the doctor can come to see one twice a day, which he cannot in the country.' When he found himself out of office he resumed work on *Endymion*, the novel he had abandoned in 1874, and with the money he received on its publication (£10,000) was able to buy himself the Curzon Street house on a nine-year lease, which he commented, 'I think will see me out.'

Though *Endymion* portrays the feelings of a dismissed and fallen statesman, Disraeli showed no signs of disillusionment. His London life, in contrast to the seclusion of Hughenden, was still active, a round of dinner parties and frequent attendance at the House of Lords, despite the fact that he was constantly struggling with illness, the winter of 1880–81 being particularly severe. In March 1881 he spoke his last words in the Lords, on the assassination of the Czar, but by the end of the month he was confined to bed suffering from bronchitis, gout and asthma. His mind was still active, however, and on 31 March he corrected the proofs of his last remarks on the address of condolence to the Queen on the Czar's death, saying: 'I will not go down to posterity as one who used bad grammar.'

Queen Victoria's continued affection for him showed in the flowers and telegrams which arrived from her daily, and during the last weeks of his illness she commanded that a layer of straw be put down in Curzon Street adjacent to Lord Beaconsfield's house, in order that he should not be disturbed by the sound of passing carriages. But at half past six in the morning of 19 April a bulletin appeared on the railings outside the house for the waiting crowd: Lord Beaconsfield had 'passed calmly away in his sleep'.

Curzon Street:
Tube: Green Park.
Bus: Nos. 2, 9, 14, 16, 19, 22, 25, 30, 36, 38, 73, 74, 137, 500.

George Eliot (Mary Ann Evans) (1819–80)

Holly Lodge, 31 Wimbledon Park Road, SW18 and 4 Cheyne Walk, SW3

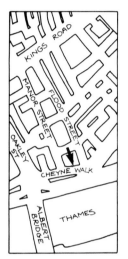

Tube: Sloane Square.
Bus: Nos. 11, 19, 22, 39, 45, 49.

In February 1859, Mary Ann Evans and George Henry Lewes, her husband in all but name, took a seven-year lease on a house in Wandsworth, Holly Lodge, Wimbledon Park Road, SW18. By this time 'George Eliot' was recognized as one of the foremost novelists of the day, having published *Amos Barton* in 1856 and *Adam Bede* in 1859. Her identity, which she and Lewes had tried to conceal, had by then been forced into the open by a Warwickshire cleric who claimed to be George Eliot. It was also now well known that she was living with Lewes, who was already married, and that they were thus openly flouting the conventions of the day.

Suburban villa

It was probably partly because of these pressures that Mary Ann (or Marian as she preferred) and Lewes decided to move to the outer suburbs. They had been lodging in Bayswater and then Richmond before coming across Holly Lodge, a solid suburban villa which Marian described as 'very comfortable . . . a tall cake with a low garnish of holly and laurel'. Holly Lodge was also near the countryside: 'We are very well off, with glorious breezy walks, and wide horizons, well-ventilated rooms, and abundant water.' They both loved to go for long walks, and would usually work in the morning, lunch at half past one, and walk in the afternoon, returning for dinner and an evening of reading aloud or listening to music. Marian was hard at work on her new novel, as she recorded in her Journal on 29 April 1859: 'Resumed my new novel . . . I shall call it provisionally *The Tullivers*, or perhaps *St Oggs on the Floss*.' The manuscript of *The Mill on the Floss* (published on 4 April 1860) bore the dedication:

> To my beloved husband, George Henry Lewes, I give the MS. of my third book, written in the sixth year of our life together at Holly Lodge, South Field, Wandsworth, and finished 21st March 1860.

She recorded that she had written the last eleven pages of the book at frantic pace: 'But I daresay there is not a word different from what it would have been if I had written them at the slowest pace.'

4 Cheyne Walk, Chelsea

Though they had envisaged Holly Lodge 'to be our dwelling, we expect, for years to come', they were very soon eager to leave. Marian found that by moving out to the suburbs they had not escaped from prying eyes and gossip, as she wrote to her publisher John Blackwood:

When Maggie [ie *The Mill on the Floss*] is done, and I have a month or two of leisure, I should like to transfer our present house, into which we were driven by haste

and economy, to someone who likes houses full of eyes all round him.

Though they entertained literary friends here, like Dickens, Wilkie Collins and Bulwer Lytton, Marian had to spend many evenings alone while Lewes dined out, as she was not socially accepted. On the other hand, they were often plagued with unwanted guests, and deliberately made their spare bedroom uncomfortable, to discourage people from staying again.

Hampered by a seven-year lease, they eventually managed to let the house in August 1860. After sixteen months in rooms at 10 Harwood Square, the couple leased 16 Blandford Square until November 1863, when they bought the Priory, 21 North Bank, NW8. This house, on the bank of the Regent's Canal in lower St John's Wood, became a focal point for literary London, where admirers came to pay court to the famous authoress, regarded, as her literary reputation increased, by all but prudes as one of the foremost moralists of the day. (All three of these London residences have since been demolished, 21 North Bank to make way for the Great Central Railway.) Marian and Lewes had always longed to leave London, however, and eventually in 1876 they purchased 'The Heights' at Witley, near Haslemere, Sussex, a house found for them by Lewes' lifelong friend, Johnny Cross.

A house in Chelsea

Only two years later, George Henry Lewes died. Marian was helped through her grief and resultant ill-health by Johnny Cross. After several proposals, she finally agreed to marry him, and on 10 April 1880 they went to look over a house in Chelsea, 4 Cheyne Walk, and decided to purchase it. Little altered today, the house is part of an impressive early Georgian terrace (nos. 3–6) built c. 1717 (the date inscribed on the lead piping of no. 4 is 1718). No. 4, faced in red brick, has a particularly fine hooded doorway, flanked by two Corinthian pilasters.

But although Marian hoped that Cheyne Walk would bring her better health as well as pleasure from the attractive surroundings, her happiness at the house was to be short-lived. The couple were married on 6 May 1880 at St Georges, Hanover Square, and after spending several months in Venice they returned to London, but did not move into their new house until 3 December. On the 18th, they attended as usual the Saturday Popular Concert, and Edmund Gosse noticed that Marian was in pain. She was, in fact, suffering from her recurrent kidney trouble: the following Wednesday she collapsed, and died the same night. 'I am left alone in this new house we meant to be so happy in', mourned Cross. George Eliot was buried in unconsecrated ground at Highgate Cemetery, near to the grave of George Henry Lewes.

Charles James Fox (1749–1806)

46 Clarges Street, W1

Charles James Fox, one of the most flamboyant figures of the eighteenth century, was born on 24 January 1749 at a house in Conduit Street, where his parents were residing temporarily while Holland House, the Jacobean mansion bought by Charles's father, underwent repair.

An unconventional upbringing

Holland House, which became the centre of intellectual society in London in the first half of the nineteenth century, was the setting of Charles's extremely unusual childhood. To say that he was indulged by his father would be an understatement. On one famous occasion, Henry Fox blew up a wall in Holland House, during Charles's absence; but so disappointed was the child to have missed the event, that on his return his father obligingly rebuilt the wall and redynamited it. His father also instilled in Charles an early passion for gambling: far from discouraging his son from the habit, when Charles was fourteen his father provided him with five guineas a night, to try his hand at Continental gaming tables. Hardly surprisingly, this turned Charles into a compulsive gambler, who on one occasion is reputed to have gambled non-stop for twenty-four hours, losing money at a rate of £10 a minute.

Despite this unconventional upbringing, Charles's innate charm and intelligence, and his early being accustomed to the company of the leading politicians and wits of the day, made him one of the most popular men of his time. This was surprising, given that he spent most of his thirty-nine-year long political career out of office, often in fierce opposition to William Pitt and George III, so that the amount of 'influence' at his disposal was minimal. Fox's London life was a constant round of political discussion and socializing. He was welcomed in the aristocratic circles at Devonshire House, Carlton House, Bedford House, and Burlington House; both a good talker and a good listener, he was also a member of Dr Johnson's exclusive 'Club', whose membership was reserved only for such illuminati 'as that if only two of them chanced to meet, they should be able to entertain each other, without wanting the addition of more company to

Tube: Green Park.
Bus: Nos. 9, 14, 19, 22, 25, 38.

pass the evening agreeably' (though Fox, as Boswell recorded with surprise, 'certainly was very shy of saying anything in Dr Johnson's presence'). Fox was also a close friend of the young Prince of Wales, introducing him to the pleasures of gambling: he even once placed a bet with the Prince, as they were walking down Bond Street together, that he would see more cats on his side of the road than the Prince on his; naturally Fox won, being fully aware that cats always preferred the sunny side of a street to the other!

Secession

As Fox grew older, however, such pleasures as London afforded lessened, and by 1786 he was settled at St Anne's Hill in Chertsey with Mrs Elizabeth Armistead, to whom he was secretly married in 1795. When, in 1793, bitterly disillusioned by the Government's conduct of war with France, Fox seceded from Parliament altogether, he and Mrs Armistead spent most of their time in this small cottage, living a bucolic existence.

Return to politics

It was his continued espousal of the cause of the French Revolution against the policy of the Government — 'How much the greatest event it is that ever happened in the World!' he had exclaimed on the taking of the Bastille — which brought Fox back into politics in 1803. He became increasingly critical of the Addington ministry's failure to preserve peace with France, and when in 1803 he took a house in Clarges Street in Mayfair it was chiefly in order to have a base for his campaign against Addington. (Clarges Street was part of a fashionable new development in the Bond Street area, and no. 46, where Fox lived briefly from 1803–4, is the original late eighteenth century building.) Fox's reluctance to be in town was manifest in a letter to his nephew in April 1804.

> I dislike it to a degree you can hardly conceive, but I feel it is right, and resolve to do it handsomely, and therefore make it a rule not even to grumble, only to you who are so far off I may.

From Clarges Street he moved to 9 Arlington Street (now demolished) on the other side of Piccadilly, which was his London residence for the last two years of his life; and though he wrote at the time 'I am not very sanguine about dispossessing the Doctor [Addington] but I had much rather the attempt should fail than that it should not have been made', he and his followers were successful. Though excluded from Pitt's new ministry on George III's express command, Fox was eventually made Foreign Secretary in 1806, and in the same year successfully moved the Act of Parliament which abolished the slave trade. He died on 13

September 1806 at the Duke of Devonshire's Chiswick House, and is buried in Westminster Abbey.

Few of Fox's many residences in London outside Clarges Street have been positively identified. Holland House, standing in the park which represents only part of the original extensive grounds, was badly damaged during the Second World War, but the east wing (c. 1640), the ground floor of the south court and the orangery can still be seen.

46 Clarges Street, from which Fox masterminded the campaign against Addington

Benjamin Franklin (1706–90)

36 Craven Street, WC2

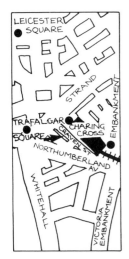

Tube: Charing Cross.
Bus: Nos. 1, 6, 9, 11, 13, 15, 77, 169, 170, 172, 176.

Benjamin Franklin was one of many visitors to London who did not find it totally congenial, especially after the relative peace and quiet of his home in Pennsylvania. As he wrote home to his wife:

> The whole town is one great smoky house and every street a chimney, the air full of floating sea coal soot, and you never get a sweet breath of what is pure without riding some miles for it into the country.

Yet Franklin spent a large proportion of his life in London. He first came to the city in 1724, when he was only eighteen, having been promised funds by Governor Keith of Pennsylvania to buy equipment to start his own printing press. Keith's funds never arrived, and Franklin worked instead for such firms as Palmer's Printing House, Watts, situated near Drury Lane, and in a print shop in what is now the lady chapel of the Church of St Bartholomew the Great, Smithfield. Franklin's exhaustive plan of self-improvement included the improvement of his literary style, and this he had achieved by the rewriting of essays from Addison's *The Spectator* and comparing them with the originals. He returned to Philadelphia in 1726 to become by 1730 the sole owner of a printing press and of the once–ailing *Pennsylvania Gazette* which he transformed into the newspaper with the largest circulation in the American colonies.

Public life

By the time Franklin returned to England in 1757 he had been married to Deborah Read for twenty-seven years and had gained a considerable reputation, both at home and abroad, based on achievements which ranged from the promotion of the Pennsylvania police force to experiments investigating the nature of electricity. He had hoped in 1748 to be able to devote all his time to his 'philosophical studies and amusements', and the results were published in *Experiments and Observations on Electricity* in 1751. But public life claimed him again, and six years later he came to England to present to Parliament the grievance of the Pennsylvania Assembly concerning the taxation of landowners.

36 Craven Street, where
Franklin lived for many
years

This matter was settled in 1760, but Franklin remained in
England.

London lodgings

He had taken lodgings, with his son William, in the house of a Mrs
Margaret Stephenson at 7 (now 36) Craven Street, off the
Strand. There he stayed during most of the period he was in
England from 1757 until 1762, and again, after a brief return to
America, between 1764 and 1775. The house is still much as it

was, although Franklin noted in 1762 that it was nearly destroyed by fire: 'Our house and yard were covered with falling coals of fire, but as it rained hard nothing catched.' It was built during the mid eighteenth century as part of a terrace of uniform houses with brick façades, three storeys above the ground floor and a basement. The iron railings and balconies are original.

Franklin seems to have been happy there. He quickly adopted the role of benevolent uncle to Mrs Stephenson's daughter Mary, continued to conduct scientific experiments, and met some of the most prominent men of the period, counting among his circle of friends such figures as Adam Smith and David Garrick. Official recognition soon followed; he received degrees of L.L.D. from St Andrews University in 1759, D.C.L. from Oxford University in 1762, and in the same year was elected a Fellow of the Royal Society. One of his most useful achievements was the discovery of the lightning conductor, and he helped to devise plans for the erection of lightning rods at St Paul's Cathedral and on the Government's powder magazine. Not surprisingly, Franklin showed little inclination to leave England, except in letters to his wife, to whom he once wrote:

'Tis true, the regard and friendship I meet with from persons of worth and the conversation of ingenious men, give me no small pleasure; but at this time of life, domestic comforts afford the most solid satisfaction, and my uneasiness at being absent from my family, and my longing desire to be with them, make me often sigh in the midst of cheerful company.

American Independence

Franklin left England in 1762 only to return two years later as agent in London for Pennsylvania. He saw his task as the reconciliation of the colonies with Britain; but he began to despair with the passing of the coercive acts in 1774, and his last months in England were spent helping Pitt in the vain search for this reconciliation. Franklin left England in March 1775.

The last years of his life included perhaps his greatest achievements. He took a major part in drafting the Declaration of Independence in 1776, was instrumental in the signing of the final peace treaty between America and Britain on 3 September 1783, served as President of the Executive Council of Pennsylvania from 1785 to 1788, and, at the age of eighty-one, took his seat in the Constitutional Convention. He died on 17 April 1790.

Sigmund Freud (1856–1939)

20 Maresfield Gardens, NW3

Sigmund Freud moved to Vienna with his parents at the age of four from Frieburg in Moravia. He lived in Vienna for the next seventy-eight years, until the annexation of Austria by Nazi Germany in 1938. Forced to flee the threatened Nazi persecution of the Jews, with the help of friends and after many months of negotiation, Freud left Vienna, and found political refuge in London.

He arrived in June 1938, and stayed for a short while at 39 Elsworthy Road, NW3, on the edge of Primrose Hill. After an operation at the London Clinic, he eventually settled at 20 Maresfield Gardens in Hampstead, little more than a mile from Elsworthy Road, in September 1938. This was to be his last residence.

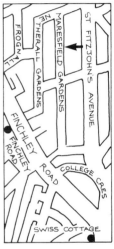

Tube: Finchley Road.
Bus: Nos. 2, 2B, 13, 113, C11.

Comfortable surroundings

The house in Maresfield Gardens is a large, dignified, many-windowed 'gentleman's residence', and provided ample and comfortable surroundings for Freud, his wife Martha, his sister-in-law, and youngest daughter Anna. By the time they moved here, their furniture and Freud's personal collections had arrived

20 Maresfield Gardens, a 'gentleman's residence'

from Vienna, and it was possible for Anna to 'reconstruct', in a room at the back of the house with french windows giving on to the pleasant tree-hung garden, a replica of Freud's study in Vienna, with all the furnishings, ornaments and pictures arranged exactly as they had been there.

Despite his age, and the knowledge that he had had cancer for the past sixteen years, Freud remained remarkably active. The upheaval of moving to London was counterbalanced by the warm welcome he was given both by the medical profession and by the general public: many letters of admiration, addressed simply to 'Freud, London', somehow reached the house. It became a meeting place for psychoanalysts, as well as an attraction for other visitors, who included Salvador Dali and H.G. Wells. Though he was often in pain, Freud continued to write: while at Elsworthy Road he produced *An Outline of Psycho-Analysis* — a restatement of his basic theories — and after the move to Maresfield Gardens he devoted himself to writing *Moses and Monotheism*, a dissertation drawing on psychoanalysis to support the theory that Moses was an Egyptian. Though he was apprehensive about producing what could be construed as an attack on Judaeism at a time of Jewish persecution, the book was published in March 1939.

That month also brought gratifying news. The twenty-fifth anniversary dinner of the British Psycho-Analytical Society was held on 10 March, and was attended by most of the eminent members of the medical profession of the day. This mark of official recognition, so long-awaited, was a far cry from the hostility with which Freud's theories had initially been greeted.

Cruel process

However, this triumph came at a sad moment, for the same month also brought the verdict that a new cancerous swelling in Freud's mouth was inoperable. He lived on for a further six months, in almost constant pain, but refusing to take any drugs other than aspirins to relieve the suffering, though confiding to a friend: 'Some kind of intervention that would cut short this cruel process would be very welcome.' His bed was moved down to his study, where Anna nursed him day and night, and where he continued to see his few patients until only a few weeks before his death.

Shortly after the outbreak of war was announced, Freud's doctor, Schur, asked him whether he agreed that this would be 'the war to end all wars'. 'My last war', Freud replied. A few weeks later, on 23 September, he died. The house remained in the family, and was lived in for many years by Anna Freud, herself a leading psychoanalyst.

Kate Greenaway (1846–1901)

39 Frognal, NW3

Kate Greenaway's solid suburban villa in Hampstead, known as Greenaway House, was built for her in 1885 by Norman Shaw, when she was at the height of her success as a writer and illustrator of children's books.

Born in 1846 at 1 Cavendish Street, Hoxton, N1, Kate Greenaway grew up in the Highbury and Islington area. Her father John, a draughtsman and engraver, encouraged his daughter's early signs of artistic talent, and at the age of twelve she was sent to the National Art Training School at the new South Kensington Museum (now the Royal College of Art). She spent ten years there, and after she left the number of commissions she received gradually increased, until in 1878 her first book, *Under the Window*, was published. Though she had already illustrated many books by other people, this was the first time that she had illustrated her own ideas, giving her new scope to experiment with the fresh, original style which became her hallmark. The publisher, Edmund Evans, gambled by printing twenty thousand copies of the book — a large quantity even today, but phenomenally large at the time. But the book sold astonishingly well, and so confident were Kate and her publisher that there was a first printing of 150,000 for her next book, *Kate Greenaway's Birthday Book for Children*.

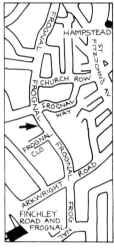

Tube: Finchley Road or Hampstead.
Bus: Nos. 2, 2B, 13, 113, C11.

Quiet life

Throughout her rise to fame and success, Kate continued to live a quiet life at home with her parents, living at 147 Upper Street, Islington, N1, from 1853–78, and thence moving to 11 Pemberton Gardens in Upper Holloway, where the family lived until 1885. Both these houses are still standing, though they do not bear plaques, which is perhaps a pity, since the latter house in particular is in an area which now has little else to recommend it, though it was once highly respectable (Holloway was the abode of Mr Pooter in *The Diary of a Nobody*).

Shortly after the publication of the *Language of Flowers*, perhaps her best-loved book, Kate Greenaway, her parents and brother John moved to the new house in Frognal, a quiet part of Hampstead which until the nineteenth century had been a village

on its own. She was severely castigated for the move by John Ruskin, her mentor and lifelong friend, who wrote to her in mock horror:

> I am aghast at the house at Hampstead and quite
> resolved that you *shan't* live in London... wait till I come
> and talk to you — I'll make your life a burden to you if
> you live in London! If you had come to Norwood [a
> southern suburb] instead of Hampstead, there would
> have been some sense in it — I've no patience with you.

A sketch from *Kate Greenaway's Book of Games*

However, Kate took little notice, and the move seems to have been a success. The new house was congenial to her, having the 'prettiness' in appearance which reflected her own taste and work. It also had a larger, lighter and 'altogether more practical' studio than she had had previously, and she could work there undisturbed. She produced many further books here, including *Marigold Garden, The Queen of the Pirate Isle, The Pied Piper of Hamelin* (an illustrated version of Browning's poem), and *The Kate Greenaway Book of Games.* Her life was one of quiet, industrious routine; she would apparently work in the morning from eight until one, continue for an hour or two in the afternoon, then walk on Hampstead Heath, returning for tea. The evenings, her brother John tells us,

> were spent in letter-writing, making dresses for models,
> occasionally working out schemes and rough sketches for
> projected books and such-like things . . . In the summer
> too, a good deal of this time was spent in the garden
> seeing to her flowers. After supper she generally lay on a
> sofa and read until she went to bed at about ten o'clock.

Although, in the 1890s, Kate Greenaway produced no more books, she held several exhibitions of her original drawings, which proved enormously popular. In 1889 she was elected a member of the Royal Institute of Painters in Water-Colours, to which she made frequent contributions of paintings and designs. Saddened by the death of Ruskin in January 1900, she died on 6 November 1901.

Opposite: 39 Frognal, designed by Norman Shaw

Georg Friedrich Handel (1685–1759)

25 Brook Street, W1

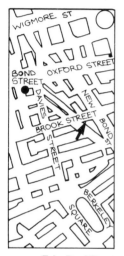

Tube: Bond Street.
Bus: Nos. 1, 3, 6, 7, 8, 12, 13,
15, 25, 53, 73, 88, 113, 137,
159.

It was in 1710 that Handel first came to England, shortly after his appointment as Kapellmeister to the Elector of Hanover. It seems that he took London by storm, especially after the production of his opera *Rinaldo*, an event which firmly established Italian opera in England. Understandably Handel, not long after his return to Hanover, asked the Elector for permission to go back to England. His request was granted, on the understanding that his stay there would be short; in fact, Handel stayed in England for forty-seven years!

Patronage

As he had probably anticipated, Handel was not short of patrons in England, which was fortunate at a time when patronage was so important to the success of a composer. For a time he lived at Burlington House, where he met many fellow artists, authors and wits of the day, though his enjoyment of such company was probably hampered by his complete inability, then and throughout his life, to come to grips with the English language. The Duke of Chandos became his chief patron, and at Canons, the Duke's residence in Edgware (now the famous North London Collegiate School) Handel composed his first oratorio *Esther* and later the *Largo*. He seems to have been somewhat alarmed when, on the death of Queen Anne in 1713, his erstwhile employer the Elector of Hanover became George I of England, and the popular theory is that Handel composed the *Water Music*, for a royal trip on the Thames, in order to regain the King's favour. But this seems unlikely: if George I did feel any resentment at Handel's desertion of the Hanoverian court, he did not show it, and in fact quickly confirmed the pension of £400 a year which Handel had been receiving from Queen Anne.

In 1723, the composer purchased an elegant Queen Anne house, no. 57 (now no. 25) Brook Street, in Mayfair. Here, in the music room on the first floor, Handel wrote some of his greatest works, including the *Messiah* and *Israel in Egypt*. During the twenty-four days in which he wrote the Messiah, Handel did not leave the house, being brought food by a servant. He was found in tears when he had finished Part II, and apparently said 'I did

think I did see all heaven before me, and the great God himself.'

Handel's fortunes had flagged during the 1730s. Though operas were generally well supported, he had often to play to empty houses, and hostility from a rival opera group led him in 1737 to bankruptcy and illness. The *Messiah*, first performed in 1741, revived his fortunes. Initially it was not well received, despite the fact that George II was so affected by the music that he rose to his feet at the beginning of the Hallelujah chorus, which audiences have done ever since. However, the work gradually achieved popularity, largely because it came to be associated with charitable causes, particularly that of the Foundling Hospital. Like Hogarth, Handel was a governor and benefactor of the Hospital (now mostly demolished) in Mecklenbergh Square in Bloomsbury; he conducted many services as well as his oratorios there, persuading other musicians to give free performances, and left the Hospital the score of the *Messiah* in his will.

25 Brook Street, where Handel composed the *Messiah* in twenty-four days

A sense of humour

Handel died a rich man, and throughout his difficulties, both financial and physical (by May 1752 he was almost blind), seems to have retained his dry sense of humour and his warmth of personality. The decoration at the house in Brook Street was very spartan, but he spared little expense where food and wine, his great loves, were concerned, and gave frequent dinner parties. At one such soirée, however, it seems he was not totally willing to share these pleasures. He suddenly exclaimed 'Oh, I haf de thought' and the guests, not wishing to disturb the great man's inspiration, urged him to withdraw to another room to set down these thoughts. During the evening, these thoughts apparently became increasingly frequent, and it was eventually discovered that they were being bestowed upon a superior wine which he did not wish to share with his guests!

Handel's last years were spent living and working in Brook Street where, on 14 April 1759, he died, only a few days after attending a performance of the *Messiah*. 25 Brook Street remains much as it was in 1759, although late in the nineteenth century an extra floor was added and, in 1906, the ground floor was converted into a shop. Between the wars there was an attempt to raise money to make the house London's Handel Museum. Unfortunately, only £250 was raised, and the scheme was abandoned.

Thomas Hardy (1840–1928)

172 Trinity Road, SW17

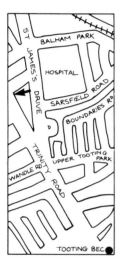

Tube: Tooting Bec.
Bus: Nos. 19, 49, 249.

Hardy first moved to London from his native Dorset in 1862. At that time, he had no serious plans of becoming a writer: his purpose in coming to London was to advance his career as an architect. Unassured of success, he had bought a return ticket in readiness for a retreat home; but luckily he found work with the distinguished architect Blomfield, who had offices in the Adelphi, the grandiose terrace built by the brothers Adam. The lively and cultivated young men who became Hardy's colleagues were worlds apart from the serious, shy and self-educated Hardy, but he soon entered into the spirit of things, cheerfully recording how he and the others would irreverently pencil caricatures on the Adams' white marble mantelpieces. He loved the cheerful surroundings of the West End, and the bustle of the docks which, even as late as this, stood on the Thames below the Adelphi.

Mechanical existence

However, Hardy missed the stability of home life. His lodgings were congenial enough: having lived for a while in Kilburn, he moved to no. 16 Westbourne Park Villas, W2, near enough for him to walk to work, in 1863. Now overshadowed by the noisy Westway, this part of Paddington was then a quiet and select area, not the land of lodging houses it later became; no. 16 was a pleasant, countrified, semi-detached villa, where lodgers were not usually accepted. But Hardy described his life as 'the fitful yet mechanical existence that befalls many a young man in London lodgings'; and, perhaps following a failed love affair recorded in the powerful poem *Neutral Tones* written at Westbourne Park Villas in 1867, in that year he returned home to Bockhampton in Dorset.

By the time he next came to live in London, Hardy had several published novels to his name, including *Far From the Madding Crowd* published in 1875, which brought him recognition for the first time. Since their marriage in 1876, he and Emma had lived in the West Country, first at Yeovil and then at Sturminster Newton. But the strain of organizing his literary affairs from such a distance led Hardy to bring Emma to London in 1878, where they signed a three-year lease on a suburban villa, 1 Arundel Terrace,

172 Trinity Road, the
Hardys' suburban home

Trinity Road, Tooting (now 172 Trinity Road). Trinity Road, a
long, straight avenue, lay pleasantly close to Wandsworth Common,
and the house was convenient for Wandsworth Common Station,
on one of the recently constructed railway lines that had so
dramatically effected the growth of the suburbs. Arundel Terrace
was a standard three-storey row of eight yellow brick villas, with
half basements and bow-windowed front parlours, and the Hardys'
house stood at one end.

Troubles

Hardy was later to write that, after the idyll of Sturminster
Newton, it was here that the troubles of his marriage began; and
although the disillusion does not seem to have been this sudden,
it was while living here that Hardy began to form the attachments
to younger and more attractive women that were to poison his
relationship with Emma. However, their troubles were partly

caused by the house itself. On the northernmost corner of the terrace and with no southern aspect, it was always cold and exposed to the vagaries of the weather, culminating in the bitter winter of 1880–81 when snow drifted in thickly through the doors and windows.

But the three years here began well. Hardy's social life advanced — Arnold and Tennyson both visited Hardy's home, and he formed a close friendship with Edmund Gosse. He lived the usual literary life, frequently visiting the theatre and dining at clubs, leaving Emma to spend many lonely evenings at home. But both the Hardys were friends of the family of the publisher Alexander Macmillan, who also lived in Tooting and with whom Hardy now renewed an acquaintance made earlier. They spent much time at the Macmillans', and Hardy's poem, *Beyond the Last Lamp (near Tooting Common)*, recalls how, on one evening visit to the Macmillans' house in Tooting Bec Road, he watched a pair of lovers endlessly pace the street outside. His glimpse of their sadness perhaps echoed his own:

> The pair seemed lovers, yet absorbed
> In mental scenes no longer orbed
> By love's young rays. Each countenance
>   As it slowly, as it sadly
>   Caught the lamplight's yellow glance,
> Held in suspense a misery
> At things which had been or might be.

Hardy's literary fortunes while in London were mixed. *The Return of the Native*, published in November 1878 though written at Sturminster, received generally bad reviews, while *The Trumpet Major*, written in London in 1879, was well reviewed but sold badly. By this time, Hardy was beginning to dislike London, reflecting morbidly that it was 'a monster with four million heads and eight million eyes'. From the back bedroom, he watched dawn break over the city: 'The roofs are damp grey, the streets are filled with night as with a dark stagnant flood whose surface brims to the tops of the houses.' He suffered increasingly from nervous and physical complaints, culminating in October 1880 in a severe internal haemorrhage. Throughout that winter he was confined to bed, although the pressures of serialization led him to dictate the remaining chapters of *A Laodicean* to Emma. It was not until early in May 1881 that he was fit enough to take a walk on Wandsworth Common. Now convinced that London was bad both for his work and for his health, Hardy returned with Emma to Dorset, where they eventually settled at the house he had built for himself, Max Gate, near Dorchester, thereby firmly rejecting the idea of making London their permanent home.

William Hogarth (1697–1764)

Hogarth House, Hogarth Lane, W4

William Hogarth was born in Bartholomew Close, in the City of
London, on 10 November 1697. The area had escaped the Great
Fire, so the Close consisted then of medieval timbered houses;
and although these were destroyed in the Blitz, the nearby
church of St Bartholomew the Great, where Hogarth was baptized,
remains little changed since it was erected in the late eleventh
century.

Smithfield

The area in which William Hogarth spent his first years was to
have a strong influence on his art. Bartholomew Close lay a few
yards east of Smithfield market: now London's most famous meat
market, it was then a market for live cattle and sheep, brought
there every morning. It was an area constantly teeming with
activity, the climax of every year being the arrival in August of
Bartholomew Fair, whose lively scenes held a strong fascination
for the young Hogarth: 'I had naturally a good eye, shews of all
sorts gave me uncommon pleasure when an Infant.' Across the
other side of the Square was St Bartholomew's Hospital, which
may account for Hogarth's continued interest in hospitals and
their works later in life.

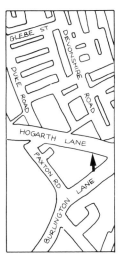

Tube: Turnham Green.
Bus: Nos. 27, 237, 267.

Leicester Fields

Hogarth showed little inclination to follow in the footsteps of his
father, who was a schoolmaster; indeed, he was probably not
encouraged by the fact that his father's fortunes were frequently
at a low ebb, so that at one point the family's only income came
from selling pots of Hogarth's mother's patent gripe ointment. It
was not altogether surprising that Hogarth escaped school early
to pursue his talent for drawing, and was apprenticed to a silver-
plate engraver in Leicester Fields (now Leicester Square). In
1720 he set himself up as an engraver in Long Lane, Smithfield,
only a few streets north of his birthplace, and there undertook
almost anything, from coats of arms to letter headings, though he
was already producing book illustrations and satirical prints. By
1724 he was successful enough to move back to the more elegant

GIN LANE

Gin Lane, one of Hogarth's best known engravings of London. *(Reproduced by kind permission of Robert Douwma Prints & Maps Ltd, London)*

surroundings of Leicester Fields, to premises on the corner of Cranbourne Alley and Little Newport Street.

By the time of his marriage to Jane Thornhill in 1729, Hogarth was established as a painter of small portrait groups, and had also enjoyed his first popular success with a scene from the *Beggar's Opera* (1728). His satirical and moral style and penchant for scenes of London life were beginning to develop, revealing a revulsion against the kind of scenes he had probably witnessed in his childhood, particularly apparent in the powerful print *Gin Lane* (1747) which showed the horrors to which addiction to gin could lead. In 1733, he was able to buy a fine house in Leicester

Hogarth's House, with the mulberry tree in the foreground. The house may be visited Mon-Sat April-October 11.00-18.00 and October-March 11.00-16.00. Closed Sunday mornings. (Tel. 01-994 6757)

Fields, which remained his town residence until his death; there he worked on *The Harlot's Progress*, the first of the series of moral paintings which were to establish him in the history of English painting as a powerful recorder of social history and a man who brought art, for the first time in England, through the mass reproduction of his paintings in engraved prints, to a large audience.

Hogarth had secured for himself a regular income without the need for patronage, and was particularly successful with his best known series *A Rake's Progress*, 1733 (now in Sir John Soane's Museum) and *Marriage à la Mode*,1743 (in the Tate Gallery);

The beautiful first-floor bay window of Hogarth's House

and it was through his pressure that the Engraver's Copyright Act was passed in 1735, protecting engravers from unscrupulous men who reproduced other engravers' prints themselves. He also tried his hand at other forms of art: for a long time he had wanted to try 'history painting', then regarded as the highest form of art, and in 1735, when he was elected a governor of St Bartholomew's Hospital, he set to work on two large murals, *The Pool of Bethesda* and *The Good Samaritan*, to adorn the Great Staircase of the Hospital (the paintings can still be seen). He continued to paint portraits, such as the portrait of the founder of the Foundling Hospital (of which Hogarth was also a governor) Sir Thomas Coram, and was allowed to use the Hospital as a permanent exhibition hall for his and other artists' works.

Chiswick

It was the practice of many successful Londoners to acquire a 'country residence', and Hogarth was no exception: in 1749 he bought a house in the village of Chiswick, on the Thames, just half a mile from Lord Burlington's Chiswick House (now, in contrast to Hogarth's, little more than a gracious shell). A small house, Hogarth's new acquisition did not quite suggest the country gentleman, but it was more substantial than the type of villa which successful tradesmen were constructing outside the City. Here he lived, with his wife and her mother and his sister Anne, until the night before his death in 1764 at his town house.

The house is lucky to have survived to the present day. By 1874 it had fallen into a state of complete disrepair, and after attempts to raise public funds to save it proved a dismal failure, it was privately bought and opened to the public in 1902, and later conveyed to Middlesex County Council on trust for use as a museum. Although it suffered severe bomb damage in 1940, it was restored and reopened by the council in 1951. It has been well restored, with a beautiful hanging bay window, and contains a fine collection of Hogarth's prints. The walled garden, where there is still growing a mulberry tree whose berries Hogarth used to give to the foundling children for whom he found homes in the village, is a peaceful contrast to the surrounding flats and factories and the busy Great West Road, now only a few yards away from Hogarth's 'little country box by the Thames'.

Henry James (1843–1916)

34 De Vere Gardens, W8

Henry James's love of London was born when, as a child of twelve, his father brought the James family on a tour of Europe. They only stayed in London for a few days, and the young Henry spent most of the time ill in a hotel bed, but he later wrote:

> I recall in particular certain short sweet times when I could be left alone — with the thick and heavy suggestions of the London room about me, the very smell of which was ancient, strange and impressive, a new revelation altogether, and the window open to the English June and the far-off hum of a thousand possibilities . . .

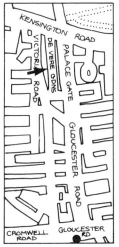

Tube: Gloucester Road or High Street Kensington.
Bus: Nos. 9, 33, 49, 52, 73.

Old World

As he grew older, his fascination for the ways of the Old World, and particularly for the London of Dickens and Thackeray, increased. He frequently toured Europe, and eventually decided in 1875 to settle in Paris. But in December 1876 he left it — he would 'be an eternal outsider' there, he felt, despite his acceptance in literary circles — and moved to London. Though he travelled a great deal, England was to be his home for the rest of his life, and he wrote most of his well known novels there. London, he wrote, 'is the biggest aggregation of human life —the most complete compendium of the world'. He even relished its constant thick fogs and persistent drizzle, unlike most of the native citizens.

James moved to De Vere Gardens, Kensington, in 1886. He had been living in lodgings at 3 Bolton Street, W1, but these rooms, though he was attached to them, were rather small and dark, and he was delighted to find the large, recently built fourth-floor flat in Kensington, with its fine views across the rooftops of the metropolis. In the same year, two of his novels, *The Bostonians* and *The Princess Casamassima*, were published. The latter revealed the one element of his adopted home that shocked James as it had shocked Dickens: the extreme poverty that pervaded even such exclusive areas as Mayfair. But the critics found fault with the book, and from then on James's writings dealt chiefly with the phenomena he observed so well — the

The doorway at 34 De Vere Gardens

contact between the New and Old Worlds, and the complexities of modern living. Among the novels he wrote at De Vere Gardens are *The Spoils of Poynton* and *The Awkward Age*. James also maintained a hectic social life here, once recording 109 dinings-out in the course of one winter!

James and the theatre

One experience which befell James while he was living here must be related. For a period in the early 1890s, he was strongly tempted by the theatre, and had several of his plays performed. Though they received a rather lukewarm reception, nothing daunted, James decided to stage his new play *Guy Domville*, and engaged the highly popular actor-manager George Alexander to play the lead.

It was not a happy event. On the opening night, James's nerves got the better of him, and he decided to steady them by going to see Oscar Wilde's *An Ideal Husband* which was being staged at the Haymarket nearby, rather than endure his own play. His forebodings grew as he listened to the laughter of the audience at Wilde's play, and was horrified to realize that the public enjoyed such frippery. He walked back gloomily afterwards across St James's Square to St James's Theatre, where *Guy Domville* was just drawing to a close as he arrived. Then, to his pleasant surprise, warm applause greeted the final curtain as he stood back-stage. Alexander, however, had been made to feel well aware during the performance that the audience were far from pleased, and that they were merely giving him his customary personal ovation. In a fit of malice, he dragged the unsuspecting James on to the stage. H.G. Wells, who was in the audience, recorded what happened:

> I have never heard any sound more devastating than the crescendo of booing that ensued. The gentle applause of the stalls was altogether overwhelmed. For a moment or so James faced the storm, his round face white above the beard, his mouth opening and shutting, and then Alexander, I hope in a contrite mood, snatched him back into the wings.

Not surprisingly, this was James's last foray into the theatrical world for some time.

Retreat

Though in the mid 1890s James moved out of London every summer, eventually buying Lamb House, Rye, Sussex (which is preserved as a museum) as a 'calm retreat', he continued to stay in London over the winter, using a permanent set of rooms at the Reform Club. After a trip to the United States in 1910 to visit his dying brother, the psychologist and philosopher William James, he felt the need to be in London and in company more often. Moreover, he was engaged in writing his autobiography (of which the third volume, *The Middle Years*, covers his life in London), and was frustrated by the fact that his secretary, being female, was not allowed into the Reform Club. So he was well pleased when, in 1913, she found for him a new London residence, 21 Carlyle Mansions, Cheyne Walk, near to her own home. It was a flat in a modern block similar to that in De Vere Gardens, and commanded a superb view over the Thames. James wrote enthusiastically: 'This Chelsea perch, the haunt of the sage and the seagull . . . proves, even after a brief experiment, just the thing for me.'

James, now over seventy, was frequently in London, especially during the War when he spent much of his time helping in London's hospitals. His sympathy with the Allied cause and irritation at the United States' refusal to enter the war led him to be naturalized in 1915, and a month before his death (in February 1916) he was awarded the Order of Merit. There is a memorial tablet to him in Chelsea Old Church, Cheyne Walk, where the funeral service was held.

Samuel Johnson (1709–84)

17 Gough Square, EC4

Tube: Blackfriars or
Chancery Lane.
Bus: Nos. 4, 6, 8, 9, 11, 15,
22, 25, 168, 171, 501, 502,
513.

Of Dr Johnson's many residences in London, the house in Gough Square is the only one still standing that can definitely be identified as his. He is known to have lived at different times in Staple Inn and in Gray's Inn, and the age of those buildings suggests that these residences may also still remain, but they have not been identified; he also lived in houses near to Gough Square, in Bolt Court and Johnson's Court.

Johnson and Fleet Street

The Gough Square house stands in the middle of the intimate complex of little courts and alleyways to the north of Fleet Street. At the time, Fleet Street itself was little different from these narrow passages: the road was only widened in 1897, when almost the entire building line of the south side of the street between Ludgate Circus and the Temple was set back considerably. In Johnson's time, the street was narrow and cobbled, and

Johnson's
chair from the Old Cock
Tavern, one of the Fleet
Street hostelries which he
frequented. The chair is
now at 17 Gough Square

17 Gough Square.
Preserved through the
generosity of Lord
Harmsworth and the
Johnson Trust, the house
contains an excellent
collection of Johnson
memorabilia, and can be
visited May-September
Mon-Sat 11.00-17.00, and
October-April Mon-Sat
11.00-16.30; closed
Sundays.

already famed for its taverns. The area was much loved by
Johnson; and perhaps no area of London is so closely linked with
one man's name as is Fleet Street with Dr Johnson. His towering
figure was frequently to be seen parading the street with his
peculiar rolling gait, his large head 'followed by his huge body in
concomitant and proportionate rhythm, while his feet appeared
to have very little to do with his motion'. He was particularly well
known at the Cheshire Cheese tavern in Wine Office Court, just
off Fleet Street; he loved nothing better than to hold forth from a
tavern chair, 'the throne of human felicity', or perhaps to withdraw to an upper room with an exclusive group of friends known
as 'The Club', who included, among others, Boswell, David
Garrick, Edmund Burke, Oliver Goldsmith and Joshua Reynolds.

The attic room at 17 Gough Square, where the *Dictionary* was compiled

If they had the energy, they would occasionally drag themselves off to the Mitre, at 39 Fleet Street (no longer standing), the tavern at which Johnson and Boswell decided upon their famous tour of the Hebrides.

Dictionary Johnson

The house in Gough Square, rented for £30 per annum, was perhaps the happiest of Johnson's London residences, and also the saddest. Something of the intense life of the house can be felt by the visitor who wanders through the homely eighteenth century rooms, and up the central wooden staircase trodden by the Doctor. He lived here from 1749–59, the years which saw him and his wife Tetty at their happiest, but which also saw her death in 1752 — the saddest event in Johnson's life.

17 Gough Square is best known, however, as the house in which Dr Johnson compiled his *Dictionary*, with which he aimed 'to secure our language from being over-run with cant, from being crowded with low terms, the spawn of folly or affectation'. The massive task took eight years to complete; but when Boswell dared to suggest that to undertake it had been rash, Johnson replied: 'I knew very well what I was undertaking — and very well how to do it — and have done it very well.' Though the task kept him in penury — he wryly defined a lexicographer in the *Dictionary* as 'a maker of dictionaries, a harmless drudge' — it was a happy time: Johnson worked together with six amanuenses in the attic which stretched right across the third floor of the house — an ideal setting for the mammoth project. At this house, Johnson also wrote his famous essays for *The Rambler* and *The Idler*, and the highly successful novel *Rasselas*. He amassed a large collection of books here, and his lesser known biographer Hawkins remembered that the books were 'chosen with so little regard to editions or their external appearances, as shewed they were intended for use, and that he disdained the ostentation of learning'.

Discord and discontent

Here also Johnson collected the curious household of people who were to remain with him for most of their lives. Even before his wife's death, and the gift of a pension from George III in 1760, he had begun to make the house a refuge for the homeless and unfortunate: these included the eccentric physician Robert Levett, a strange maid, a Negro boy named Francis Barber, and a friend of his wife's, Miss Anna Williams. It was a motley collection, and not always harmonious, as Johnson often reflected ruefully: 'There is as much malignity amongst us as can well subsist, without any thoughts of daggers and poisons . . .discord and discontent reign in my humble habitation as in the palaces of monarchs.' It was not surprising that he was increasingly anxious to escape to the tranquil home of his friends Henry Thrale, a wealthy brewer, and his wife Hester, at Streatham Park on Tooting Common, much to the annoyance of Boswell, who often came to London expressly to see Johnson only to find that his mentor had withdrawn to the country with the Thrales!

Johnson was rarely at his last home, 8 Bolt Court (now demolished) — but, though he spent more and more time in his later years travelling up and down the country, London remained dear to him; for as he once said, 'when a man is tired of London, he is tired of life, for there is in London all that life can afford'.

John Keats (1795–1821)

Keats' House (Wentworth Place), Keats Grove, NW3

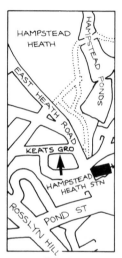

Tube: Hampstead.
Bus: Nos. 24, 46, 187, 268, C11.

Though he only spent a few years of his short life there, Hampstead was the scene of almost the whole of Keats' poetic output. His association with the north London village began in 1816. Up until then, he had been living in Southwark, where he was studying medicine at Guy's Hospital, and then in Cheapside in the heart of the City; but he was already dissatisfied with his projected career, and at the age of twenty-one was determined to be a poet — he had indeed already had a fair amount of his poetry published in periodicals. In 1816, be became acquainted with Leigh Hunt, who had published some of Keats' work and who lived in the Vale of Health, then a tiny hamlet to the north of Hampstead. Keats was drawn into Leigh Hunt's literary circle, and eventually, in March 1817, he left Guy's and moved, with his two brothers Tom and George, into lodgings at 1 Well Walk, Hampstead (now demolished), the home of the local postman. Here he wrote part of *Endymion*, the work which marked the beginning of his poetic maturity.

Wentworth Place

Then in 1818 Keats' brother George left for America, and on 1 December of that year his other brother Tom died of consumption. Shortly afterwards, Keats moved to Wentworth Place (now known as Keats' House). Though now one house, the white-stuccoed building was originally a pair of semi-detached houses, built in 1815 for two men, Charles Brown and his childhood

eighteen-year-old daughter of the family who were renting the other half of Wentworth Place from Dilke.

In the early period of their closeness, Keats wrote some of his finest poems, including the *Ode to Psyche*, the *Ode on a Grecian Urn*, and the *Ode to a Nightingale*. The latter was inspired by a nightingale who had built her nest in the garden of the house in the summer of 1819. Brown recorded the genesis of the poem:

Opposite: Wentworth Place, open to the public throughout the year Mon-Sat 10.00-13.00 and 14.00-18.00, Sun 14.00-17.00. (Tel. 01-435 2062)

Keats felt a tranquil and continual joy in her song, and one morning he took his chair from the breakfast table to the grass-plot under a plum, where he sat for two or three hours. When he came into the house, I perceived he had some scraps of paper in his hand, and these he was quietly thrusting behind the books. On inquiry, I found those scraps, four or five in number, contained his poetic feeling on the song of our nightingale. The writing was not very legible; and it was difficult to arrange the stanzas on so many scraps. With his assistance I succeeded, and this was his *Ode to a Nightingale*.

The poem seems to contain an ominous premonition of Keats' premature death:

Darkling I listen; and, for many a time
 I have been half in love with easeful Death,
Call'd him soft names in many a musèd rhyme,
 To take into the air my quiet breath;
Now more than ever seems it rich to die,
 To cease upon the midnight with no pain,
  While thou art pouring forth thy soul abroad
   In such an ecstasy!

Death warrant

Fighting against the lethargy induced by the overpowering distraction of love, Keats left Wentworth Place in the summer, as Brown always rented out the house for the summer period, and went to live in Westminster. But he found himself unable to break off his engagement to Fanny, and was back at the house for the winter. Then, in the following February, 1820, Keats found himself coughing up blood—the first sign of consumption, which had claimed both his mother and his brother Tom. He exclaimed to Brown:

I know the colour of that blood— it is arterial blood—I cannot be deceived in that colour—that drop of blood is my death warrant— I must die.

He was confined to a sofa in the front room of the house, seeing Fanny, who refused to end the engagement, as often as possible, or writing her notes:

They say I must remain confined to this room for some time. The consciousness that you love me will make a pleasant prison of the house next to yours.

Again, the following summer, Keats and Brown left the house; this time Keats took rooms in Kentish Town, then an outlying village to the south of Hampstead (this whole area was not completely built up until the 1880s), at 2 Wesleyan Place. At this

Keats painted in his sitting-room at Wentworth Place by Joseph Severn, who accompanied the poet to Italy in September 1820. *(National Portrait Gallery)*

house, which is still standing, he saw through the press *Lamia, Isabella, The Eve of St Agnes and Other Poems*, written over the previous two years. But he remained morbid, his jealous eyes 'fixed on Hampstead all day'; and one day he somehow managed to drag himself the few miles up to Hampstead, where he was spotted, a pathetic figure, 'sitting and sobbing his dying breath into a handkerchief' on a bench in Well Walk. Either then or shortly after, the Brawnes took him into their house at Wentworth Place. Fanny and her mother nursed him for a month, until on 13 September he left the house and Fanny for the last time, instructed by doctors to spend the winter in Italy. He died in Rome on 23 February 1821.

A memorial to Keats

Keats' House has been restored to be as nearly as possible as it was when Keats lived there. In 1838, the house was made into one, the extension to the left of the house being added in 1839 to make a new drawing-room. The house was finally bought by Hampstead Borough Council in 1920, and with the aid of donations (mostly from the United States) was made a memorial to Keats. It now contains many interesting literary and personal relics of the poet, Fanny Brawne and their circle, including several of Keats' annotated books, letters and personal mementoes of him and Fanny Brawne.

John F. Kennedy (1917–1963)

14 Princes Gate, SW7

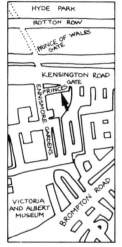

Tube: Knightsbridge.
Bus: Nos. 9, 52, 73.

Early in 1938, Joseph P. Kennedy was appointed U.S. Ambassador to Great Britain, and he, his wife Rose and their nine children moved into the house which was then the American Ambassador's residence in London: 14 Princes Gate, SW7.

It was a palatial residence, built around 1850: originally constructed as two houses, the property was bought in the early years of the twentieth century by a wealthy American banker, John Pierpoint Morgan Senior, who converted the two houses into one and made elaborate alterations to both the façade and the interior. The house passed to his son, who made it a museum and art gallery before in the early 1920s giving the building to the United States Government, who used it for many years.

Family of eleven

The house, which, apart from the servants' quarters, had eight bedrooms, was usually adequate in size to accommodate comfortably an Ambassador and his family. Not so a family of eleven, however, and Rose Kennedy consequently cut down on the number of staff in order to release some extra bedrooms for her offspring who, fortunately, were not all there all of the time. There was also the problem that the walls were bare, since the previous incumbent had given his magnificent art collection to the National Gallery in Washington. However, the Kennedys' resourcefulness secured the loan of a number of masterpieces from Randolph Hearst's castle in Wales.

The second son, John (Jack) F. Kennedy, was not always in England while his father was Ambassador. He had, in fact, already had a brief spell in London. His father was anxious that his son should spend some time at the London School of Economics under the tutelage of Professor Harold Laski: not that Joe Kennedy approved of the latter's left-wing ideas, but he felt that his son ought to be able to see life 'from both sides of the street'. Without enthusiasm, Jack enrolled in 1935, but had to drop out after a month and return to the United States because he was suffering from jaundice. He then went to Princeton to continue his studies, before having to drop out again through illness, and

The imposing entrance at 14 Princes Gate, formerly the U.S. Embassy in London

thence to Harvard, where he was studying when his family moved to England.

Crisis in Europe

For a while Jack merely joined his family in vacations, but early in 1939, when the crisis in Europe seemed to be coming to a head, Joe Kennedy decided that it would be sensible for Jack to see the events and learn from them at first hand: Jack was thus in England for much of 1939, having deferred a year at Harvard. During this time, he acted unofficially as his father's 'eyes and ears', visiting Paris, Moscow, Leningrad, Jerusalem, Warsaw and Madrid to monitor events. He, his mother, elder brother Joe and sister Kick were in the gallery at the House of Commons on 3 September 1939 when Chamberlain, a personal friend of their father's, was forced to admit the defeat of his policies of appeasement:

> Everything I have worked for, everything that I have
> hoped for, everything that I have believed in during my
> public life has crashed in ruins.

Jack left England with the rest of the family later that month, while their father stayed on as Ambassador until the end of 1940. Resuming his studies at Harvard from which he graduated *cum laude*, he produced a thesis of astonishing maturity on England's unpreparedness for the War; published as *Why England Slept*, it became a bestseller on both sides of the Atlantic, and amply revealed the great talents of the future President of the United States.

Rudyard Kipling (1865–1936)

43 Villiers Street, WC2

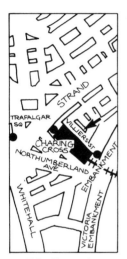

Tube: Charing Cross or Embankment.
Bus: Nos. 1, 6, 9, 11, 13, 15, 77, 168, 170, 172, 176.

G.K. Chesterton once wrote of Kipling that 'He has been to England a great many times; he has stopped there for long visits. But he does not belong to it, or to any place.' And when Kipling came to London in September 1889, at the age of twenty-three, he certainly chose an obscure and unfashionable neighbourhood in which to live: he took a dingy set of rooms which he described as 'small, not over-clean, or well-kept', in Villiers Street off the Strand. On the third storey, these two small rooms and tiny hall were decorated with assorted Oriental knick-knacks, and were constantly littered with papers and tobacco ash.

A noisy neighbourhood

Villiers Street was once described by Kipling as 'primitive and passionate in its habits and population'. It was not a street which had ever attracted the illustrious, though John Evelyn, the diarist, is believed to have lived there in 1683–84. The whole of the western side of the street had been pulled down in the 1860s to make way for Charing Cross railway station, and consequently it was a somewhat noisy neighbourhood. As Kipling remembered in his autobiography *Something of Myself*, 'the Charing Cross trains rumbled through my dreams on one side, the boom of the Strand on the other, while before my windows, Father Thames under the Shot Tower walked up and down with his traffic.' One of his windows looked on to the Embankment Gardens, with Waterloo Bridge in the distance, but the grime and smoke of the area frequently dimmed the pleasure of the view: 'Once I faced the reflection of my own face in the jet-black mirror of the window panes for five days.'

Kipling was not an unknown writer when he arrived in England in 1889. The reputation he had quickly established as a writer of verse and short stories while working as a journalist in India and America preceded him, and he was soon besieged by editors eager to bring his works written in India to the attention of the British public. He began to work seemingly tirelessly, often till two or three in the morning, with no fear of writing himself out. He wrote at a large desk between his two windows, usually dressed oddly in a loose, high-buttoned suit and a scarlet fez, and on the

43 Villiers Street (now
Kipling House) where
Kipling had rooms on the
third floor

door he had pasted a sign TO PUBLISHERS: A CLASSIC WHILE YOU WAIT!
While at Villiers Street he wrote some of his best known works,
including the *Barrack Room Ballads*, many short stories, and also
a largely autobiographical novel *The Light that Failed*, which
alone among the works he wrote there was a rather unsuccessful
piece of writing.

Portrait of Kipling by
Sir Philip Burne-Jones,
1899. *(National Portrait
Gallery)*

Time alone

Despite having rapidly achieved fame, Kipling's life in London
was quiet, and indeed, often lonely, largely as a result of his own
distrust of the literary world. Although he had been elected a
member of the Savile Club in 1890, after being nominated by
some of the best known literati of the day, he tried to avoid the
Club as much as possible, and showed little interest in meeting
other writers. The only strong friendship he formed during his
stay in London was with the young American Wolcott Balestier,
whose sister Caroline Kipling married in January 1892 at All
Souls, Langham Place.

So Kipling spent quite a proportion of his time alone, or in the
company of relatives and childhood friends, particularly 'Aunt
Georgie' and the artist Edward Burne-Jones, with whom he had
often stayed as a child at The Grange in North End Road to
escape from the elderly relatives who brought him up at what he
called the 'House of Desolation' in Southsea. He would often
pass the afternoon with the Burne-Jones's, then dine at one of the
restaurants which lined the Strand, and spend the evening alone.
'Never was life so utterly isolated. I must confess I enjoy it,
though there are times when I feel utterly lonely. But then I can
watch the fire, and weave tales, and dream dreams.' He was often
short of money—he came to London with only £200, and despite
his quick success hard cash was often lacking. Fortunately,
Villiers Street then, as now, was a home of cheap food establishments, and below Kipling's rooms were the premises of Harris
the Sausage King, 'who for tuppence gave as much sausage as
would carry one from breakfast to dinner'. When he had the
princely sum of fourpence to spare he would frequent Gatti's
Music Hall across the street under the railway arches, where he
enjoyed 'the smoke, the roar and the good-fellowship of relaxed
humanity' and of course the music—an atmosphere vividly
recorded in the *Barrack Room Ballads*.

Kipling left London and Villiers Street in June 1891, at the
instigation of his parents and doctor; his health had broken down
after a bout of influenza, when 'all my Indian microbes joined
hands and sang for a month in the darkness of Villiers Street'.
Besides this, those whose opinions he valued, such as Edmund
Gosse and Robert Louis Stevenson, were warning him that he
had saturated the market and needed to refuel his creative
energies by travelling: 'He is all smart journalism and cleverness'
wrote Stevenson, 'it is all bright and shallow and limpid'. Eventually Kipling and his wife lived in New England, where he wrote
The Jungle Book, Captain Courageous and *Many Inventions*.
They finally settled in England, having bought 'Batemans' in
Burwash, Sussex, which remained Kipling's home until his death
on 18 January 1936.

T.E. Lawrence (of Arabia) (1888–1935)

14 Barton Street, SW1

At the beginning of 1922, T.E. Lawrence moved into the attic of 14 Barton Street, a house which was the office of his friend, the architect Sir Herbert Baker. He lived there for some months, before leaving to enlist in the R.A.F. in August 1922, though he continued to use Barton Street as an occasional residence and forwarding address until 1928.

Mental breakdown

His stay here was a time of mental crisis for Lawrence — reflecting afterwards on these months, he was to comment: 'I

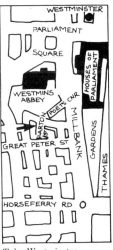

Tube: Westminster.
Bus: Nos. 3, 77, 159, 168.

The house in Barton Street, where Lawrence lived for some months in 1922, is in an area of exceptional architectural interest: Barton Street and nearby Little College Street and Lord North Street are some of the most perfectly preserved early Georgian streets in London. Nos. 1-14 Barton Street, apart from nos. 2 and 8, are all the original houses, built in 1722

Barton Street is one of the few areas of London still lit by gas lamps

think I had a mental breakdown.' Outwardly, he was a successful diplomat, having in 1921 secured Arab rule in both Transjordan and Iraq as Churchill's official adviser at the Middle East Department. But inwardly, he was bitterly disillusioned with his 'success' and fame: Lawrence of Arabia to him was little more than a fraud, who, despite his claims and efforts during the war to free the Arabs from Turkish control, had in the end failed to secure self-government for the Middle East: 'I failed badly in attempting a piece of work which a little more resolution would have pushed through, or left untouched.' The Middle East carve-up of 1919 seemed to give the lie to his whole purpose throughout the war, and the concessions of 1921 seemed a poor compromise.

Much of Lawrence's time at Barton Street was now spent working on the account of his experiences, *The Seven Pillars of Wisdom*. While in Paris for the 1919 Peace Conference he had worked frantically hard on the book to assuage his frustration with the diplomats, writing as much as 30,000 words in twenty-four hours, and he had finished the first draft by August 1919. Back in England, where he lived for a while as a Fellow of All Souls College, Oxford, he continued to work on the draft, only to lose the entire manuscript while changing trains at Reading Station. While at Barton Street, to which he came partly to escape from publicity, he was still working on the second version of the book. He lived a hermit-like existence, sleeping by day and working on the manuscript at night, usually eating at railway stations and spending the occasional night in a hotel when his clothes needed to be washed.

Lawrence's decision to join the R.A.F. under the name of J.H. Ross was brought about partly by his severe depression. He wrote to his mother morbidly that life at Barton Street was 'altogether too pleasant to be allowed to go on for long'; his deep sense of failure made him feel ashamed to be happy, and his craving for anonymity led him to join the R.A.F. as an aircraftman.

Flight from fame

The last years of Lawrence's life were on the whole unhappy ones, a perpetual flight from his undesired fame. Discharged from the R.A.F. after his identity became known, Lawrence sought refuge in the Tank Corps, but was later able to rejoin the R.A.F. In 1927 he changed his name by deed poll to T.E. Shaw. In March 1935 he retired from the R.A.F. and went to live at his cottage, Clouds Hill at Bovington, Dorset. Two months later he was dead, killed on 13 May 1935 when, swerving to avoid some children, his beloved Brough Superior motorcycle hurtled off the road.

Karl Marx (1818–83)

28 Dean Street, W1

In 1849, as a result of his inflammatory activities during the revolutions of 1848, Karl Marx was expelled from Prussia. He brought his family to London, where he remained for the rest of his life.

After staying for a while in Camberwell, Marx and his family moved to no. 64 Dean Street in May 1850. (This house has since been demolished.) Shortly afterwards, in December, they moved to no. 28, where they took two small rooms on the first floor. The house, which is of four storeys and three bays wide, was built c. 1734, and had once been an elegant town house in what was in the eighteenth century a prestigious residential area, part of the new Portland Estate. (An unusual number of houses dating from the

Tube: Tottenham Court Road.
Bus: Nos. 1, 14, 19, 22, 24, 29, 38, 176.

28 Dean Street: the Marxes are thought to have lodged on the first floor

1730s and 1740s have survived in Dean Street.) But by the mid nineteenth century, this part of Soho was a virtual slum, the home of transients then as now. Marx was one of several exiles from the turbulence of Europe at this time to settle in the area.

The awfulness of existence

The six years Marx spent at 28 Dean Street marked the nadir of his life, both privately and publicly. Once relatively wealthy, Marx and his family were now almost destitute. While they were here, though Marx contributed some articles to newspapers and periodicals — he was European Economics Correspondent of the *New York Tribune* — the income from his writing was meagre and spasmodic, so he relied almost wholly on the charity of Engels, who was fortunate enough to be the son of a Manchester factory-owner. The family had never before known such poverty, and the consequent sickness caused the death of three of the Marxes' six children at Dean Street. Jenny Marx later recounted the harrowing tale of how, when their baby Francesca died, the Marxes had to borrow money to pay for a coffin:

> The dear child's death came at the time of our bitterest
> poverty. I ran to a French refugee who lived
> nearby . . . He showed the greatest sympathy and gave
> me two pounds. With these we bought the little coffin in
> which my poor child now slumbers in peace. The child
> had no cradle when she came into the world, and this last
> little dwelling was long denied her.

Marx, despite frequent sickness, would spend most days working in the British Museum (he was at the time preparing material for the first volume of *Das Kapital*, published in 1859), returning at night to write. Sometimes, however, he was unable to leave the house, as his clothes were at the pawnshop. But despite the 'awfulness of existence' and the overcrowding, the Marxes' two rooms often put up refugees and sympathizers for the night. A Prussian agent who visited them wrote in amazement:

> . . . in the apartment there is not one clean and good
> piece of furniture to be found: all is broken, tattered and
> torn, everywhere clings thick dust, everywhere is in the
> greatest disorder . . . But all this gives Marx and his wife
> not the slightest embarrassment; one is received in the
> friendliest way.

Marx was also at the lowest point of his public influence. Marx and Engels' realization that the revolutionary period had been transient led them to break with the Communist League, whose members still hoped for continued revolution. However, the consequent isolation gave Marx a new freedom to develop his ideas away from the activists, and to engross himself in economics in preparation for *Das Kapital*. 'If one approaches him one is greeted with economic expressions instead of salutations' complained a friend.

Inheritance

In 1856 a small inheritance from Jenny Marx's uncle enabled the family to leave the poor quarter and to rent a house at 9 (now 46) Grafton Terrace in Kentish Town, NW5 and from there with the aid of another inheritance in 1863 they moved to 1 Modena Villas (now 1 Maitland Park Road, NW3) in the same area. But they were still poor: even when they received windfalls, they were too accustomed to bourgeois existence to be careful with money. Jenny suffered terribly, and Marx wrote:

> Every day my wife tells me she wishes she and the
> children were dead and buried. And really I cannot argue
> with her. For the humiliation, torments and terrors that
> have to be gone through in this situation are really
> indescribable . . .

The Marxes were eventually freed from their previous worries in 1869, when Engels sold out of his father's firm and was able to grant Marx a permanent income of £350 per year. The family moved to no. 41 Maitland Park Road in 1875 (destroyed in the Blitz) where their life became comparatively calm. Marx continued to study in the British Museum for the second and third volumes of *Das Kapital*. But he was unable to complete the work: his failing health prevented him from following his routine of sixteen hours' work a day. After his wife's death in 1881 he wandered the continent in search of health, but died in March 1883 at Maitland Park Road, and was buried in Highgate Cemetery.

Controversy

Though 46 Grafton Terrace and 1 Maitland Park Road are still standing, the G.L.C. decided that a plaque at 28 Dean Street would best commemorate Marx's life in London. Erected in 1967, the plaque was not welcomed by many who regarded Marx as too controversial a figure to receive such an honour. One who was not entirely happy with the scheme was Peppino Leoni, then owner of the *Quo Vadis* restaurant (which now occupies the ground floor of no. 28) who complained:

> My clientele is the very best . . . rich people . . . nobility
> and royalty — and Marx was the person who wanted to
> get rid of them all!

William Morris (1834–96)

17 Red Lion Square, WC1
and Red House, Red House Lane, Bexley Heath

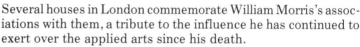

Red Lion Square:
Tube: Holborn.
Bus: Nos. 5, 7, 8, 19, 22, 25, 38, 55, 172, 501.

Several houses in London commemorate William Morris's associations with them, a tribute to the influence he has continued to exert over the applied arts since his death.

Williams's childhood was spent largely in Walthamstow, then a quiet village overlooking the Lea Valley, and set on the edge of Epping Forest. (Water House, the Georgian mansion which was the family home from 1848–56, is now the William Morris Gallery.) After a period at Exeter College, Oxford, where he quickly established the close friendship with Edward Burne-Jones which was to endure throughout their lives, Morris moved to London, when the architect for whom he worked after leaving the University transferred his practice from Oxford to the capital. Morris and Burne-Jones, who was already in London studying art under Rossetti, decided to share rooms, and after a short stay in Bloomsbury they took over the unfurnished rooms at 17 Red Lion Square which had previously been occupied by Rossetti. They stayed there from 1856 until 1859.

Medieval furniture

It was the problem of providing furniture for these rooms that first led William Morris to try his hand at furniture design. Ever since his childhood days at Woodford Hall, a Palladian mansion in the heart of Epping Forest where the Morris family had lived a semi-medieval existence, Morris had had a passion for things medieval, which was encouraged by the Victorian cult of the Middle Ages begun by Carlyle. Now, Rossetti reported, Morris was having some 'intensely medieval furniture' made — 'tables and chairs like incubi and succubi'. The experience of furniture design spurred Morris's interest in the applied arts, coming at a time when he had decided to abandon architecture and also that he was not talented enough to be a fine artist like Burne-Jones. His early attempts at design at Red Lion Square were impressive; however, the end result was not always exactly what he had planned it to be, a fact which frequently caused amusement, particularly in the case of a large settle which he had designed. Burne-Jones remembered:

17 Red Lion Square

There were many scenes with the carpenter, especially I
remember the night when the settle came home. We
were out when it reached the house, but when we came
in, all the passages and the staircase were choked with
vast blocks of timber, and there was a scene. I think the
measurements had perhaps been given a little wrongly,
and that it was bigger altogether than he had ever meant,
but set up it was finally, and our studio was one-third
less in size.

The atmosphere of the flat was never one of effete aestheticism,
as the image of the Pre-Raphaelites might suggest. Red Lion
Mary, the valiant housekeeper, struggled to keep the place in
order and to avoid the two lodgers' interminable practical jokes,
while managing to accommodate the stream of visitors, as Georg-
iana, Burne-Jones' future wife, recalled:

She cheerfully spread mattresses on the floor for friends
who stayed there, and when the mattresses came to an
end it was said that she built up beds with boots and
portmanteaux.

A new style of architecture

It was when Morris married Jane Burden, the Pre-Raphaelites'
favourite model, that he decided to leave this Bohemian existence
behind him and to settle into a house. Still possessing considerable wealth as a result of his father's successful speculation in
shares, he asked the architect Philip Webb, a friend from his days
in an architect's office, to design a home for him. Morris bought a
plot of land in Bexley Heath, and the house Webb designed, Red
House, proved to be a landmark in domestic architecture, a
rejection of the fussy classical conventions of the day in favour of
a simple, medieval-based style of architecture. Deriving its name
from the brick fabric and red roofs, it was a large, L-shaped, two-
storeyed house, whose projecting porches and bays, varying roof
lines and tall chimney stacks made it totally different from
anything else in London. It was, of course, to set a new trend for
the red brick and Tudor-style 'cottages' of developing suburbia.
Now itself in the heart of a south London suburb, it then stood in
its own orchard, commanding wide views over the Cray valley.

Morris and the Pre-Raphaelite circle set to work to decorate
the house in an appropriate style, to create, in Rossetti's words,
'more of a poem than a house . . . but an admirable place to live in
too'. It was to be a vehicle for the expression of their own
particular taste, from the plain-tiled floors and simple staircase
to Burne-Jones' paintings of medieval scenes on the drawing-
room walls and Morris's own stained-glass windows, and the
result can still be admired today, as much of the original furniture
and decoration still exists. It is of particular interest, as the Red

Red House, Bexley Heath.
The house may be visited
on the first Sunday of every
month, from 14.30-16.30, by
arrangement with the owner

Red House:
Rail: Bexleyheath
(overground from Cannon
Street, Charing Cross,
London Bridge or
Waterloo).
Bus: Nos. 89, 96, 122, 132.

House venture gave Morris and friends 'the idea... of putting our experience together for the service of the public', and led him directly to the foundation of the firm Morris, Marshall, Faulkner and Co in 1861, in which most of the Pre-Raphaelite circle had a share. The firm aimed to foster a new appreciation of the fine arts, and designed and produced furniture, wallpaper, stained glass and metal ware, later extending to complete schemes of decoration.

End of a chapter

Morris spent five years in the idyllic setting of Red House, but in 1865 decided to move back to central London in order to pursue his work more effectively; he and Jane lodged above the firm's premises in Queen Square, WC1 (formerly no. 26, now demolished). The move ended a chapter of Morris's life: his re-created medieval existence and the happy early years of his marriage were now over. Never well matched, the Morrises now drifted further apart, and the failure of their marriage was sealed by Jane's passionate attachment to and eventual affair with Rossetti. Morris's growing despair at the turn of events pervades the first volume of his poem *The Earthly Paradise*, published in 1868. However, the firm was thriving, and receiving many important commissions, one of which was to design the Green Dining Room (which may still be seen) at the Victoria and Albert Museum.

After living for a while in Oxfordshire at Kelmscott Manor and then at Chiswick (when Rossetti moved to the Manor to be with Jane), Morris eventually settled at Kelmscott House, 26 Upper Mall, W 6 in 1878, where he lived until his death. This house, built in the 1780s, is now the headquarters of the William Morris Society, and it was here that Morris founded the Kelmscott Press in 1891, a publishing firm devoted to the printing and binding of fine books, most of them designed by Morris himself.

The Green Dining Room at the Victoria and Albert Museum, designed by Morris, Marshall, Faulkner and Co. *(V & A)*

Pioneer

Morris's contribution to the architecture of London is not only evident in the tradition he inspired. In 1877, he and his friends set up the Society for the Protection of Ancient Buildings, with the aim of preventing the so-called restoration, favoured by George Gilbert Scott and others, of old buildings, which frequently amounted to virtual rebuilding, usually to detrimental effect. Morris and his friends were the first to campaign for the *conservation* of buildings, and they were instrumental in preventing many 'restoration' schemes — for instance, a plan to add to Westminster Abbey, and to rebuild Westminster Hall in 'Norman' style. That the Society still exists and is extremely influential is a tribute to Morris's pioneering spirit.

Wolfgang Amadeus Mozart (1756–91)

180 Ebury Street, SW1

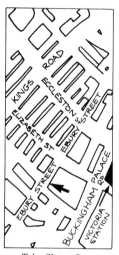

Tube: Sloane Square or Victoria.
Bus: Nos. 10, 11, 16, 25, 38, 39, 52, 137, 149, 500, 503, 507.

Mozart's one and only visit to London was as a child of eight. His father Leopold, court musician to the Archbishop of Salzburg, realizing that he had two extraordinary prodigies on his hands in the shape of his son Wolfgang and daughter Nannerl, had decided to capitalize on their musical talents by conducting them on a tour of Europe. By the time they reached London in April 1764, they had been all over Germany, to Vienna and then Paris, where they had been enthusiastically received by Louis XV at Versailles. Their hopes of London were high, as London was then the musical capital of Europe: Handel, who had spent most of his life there, had died five years previously, and J.C. Bach was at this time music master to George III and Queen Charlotte.

Royal acclaim

The Mozarts' hopes were not disappointed. Within five days of their arrival, they were summoned to Court, and were given a gratifying welcome at St James's. To George III's delight, the young Wolfgang played the King's favourite works by Handel and J.C. Bach at sight. Captivated, the King and Queen made the

The Rotunda at Ranelagh Gardens, where Wolfgang and Nannerl gave one of many successful concerts.
(National Gallery)

family return frequently. J.C. Bach, much impressed by the child, became a firm friend; when Wolfgang came to Court, he would often take the child on his knee, and the two would play together for hours.

Wolfgang and Nannerl were soon giving public concerts, and on 29 June played a highly successful concert for charity in the Rotunda at Ranelagh Gardens in Chelsea, one of London's renowned pleasure grounds by the Thames. Advertisements for the concert were sure to attract attention to the astonishing prodigy:

> The celebrated child and astonishing Master MOZART, lately arrived, a Child of 7 years of Age, will perform several select Pieces of his own Composition on the Harpsichord and on the Organ, which has already given the highest Pleasure, Delight and Surprize to the greatest Judges of Music in England or Italy, and is justly esteemed the most extraordinary Prodigy, the most amazing Genius that has appeared in any Age.

On their arrival, the family had first taken lodgings at Cecil Court, St Martin's Lane, with a Mr John Couzens, a hairdresser. Soon afterwards, they moved to Thrift (now Frith) Street in Soho,

180 Ebury Street, where Mozart composed his first symphony

taking lodgings over a shop. From here Leopold advertised that the family would be at home from twelve until two o'clock every day, so that any sceptic who doubted Wolfgang's age or true ability could come and check the authenticity of the prodigy for himself. Predictably, the child's ability had led to rumours that he was far older than his father claimed; eventually, a distinguished musician and lawyer subjected the boy to a series of tests, and in 1770 reported to no less a body than the Royal Society that Wolfgang had indeed been eight years old at the time of his visit.

Mozart's first symphony

During the summer of 1764, Leopold became very ill, and the family decided to move to the country for seven weeks, choosing Chelsea, then a quiet little village, as a suitable spot. They took lodgings in a doctor's house in Five Fields Row (now 180 Ebury Street). The house and surrounding area were a pleasing contrast to Thrift Street; the gracious, recently built house possessed a large garden, and as Leopold commented, 'It has one of the most beautiful views in the world. Wherever I turn my eyes, I only see gardens, and in the distance the finest castles.'

It was here that Wolfgang, with the aid of Nannerl, composed his first symphony (K16). Because their father needed complete rest and quiet, all musical instruments were forbidden to the children — so they spent their time composing. As well as the first symphony, Mozart also wrote another here (K19), and various short pieces, collected in an album known as the *Chelsea Notebook*. When, in November, Wolfgang presented Queen Charlotte with the works he had written while at Five Fields Row, she was so impressed that she gave him fifty guineas.

180 Ebury Street looks today much as it did in the mid eighteenth century — indeed the row 180–88 are all original houses. The seven weeks spent here were probably Wolfgang's happiest times in London, light relief doubtless being provided by trips to the famous Chelsea Bun House just around the corner.

During the winter, however, the popularity of the prodigies began to fade; as with any other curiosity, the novelty soon wore off. The family had to move from the elegant but expensive West End to the City as their income declined, and Wolfgang began to give daily performances between twelve and three o'clock at the Swan and Hoop Inn in Cornhill, where the family was lodging. They finally left London in July 1765, but Mozart long cherished an affection for the city stronger than for any other place: he had doubtless seen all the sights of the city such as the Tower, Westminster Abbey, St Paul's, and the Royal Exchange with the wondering eyes of a child. Unfortunately, he was never able to return.

Horatio, Viscount Nelson (1758–1805)

103 New Bond Street, W1

Though only thirty-nine when he lived at 103 New Bond Street during the winter of 1797–98, Nelson was already a formidable figure in the British navy. Earlier in 1797 he had had his first experience of a major battle at Cape St Vincent, where his audacious tactics seized the imagination of the British fleet and of the nation at home. After this triumph, however, had come the disastrous expedition to Santa Cruz in Tenerife, during which Nelson lost his right arm.

When Nelson returned to England in September 1797, after an absence of four years, he was thus on leave for convalescence, which proved to be long and painful. His contemporary biographer Southey tells us that 'He had scarcely any intermission of pain, day or night, for three months after his return to England.' After joining his wife Fanny in Bath, they travelled to London, which Nelson preferred to their quiet cottage in his native Norfolk, and took lodgings in fashionable New Bond Street. Though Nelson lived in a number of London houses, 103 New Bond Street is believed to be the only surviving house in which he stayed; it is a large four-storey building, and the proportion and distribution of its windows suggest that it dates from the late eighteenth century, although New Bond Street was begun in the 1720s.

Tube: Bond Street.
Bus: Nos. 1, 6, 7, 8, 12, 13, 15, 25, 73, 88, 113, 137, 159, 500, 616.

A national hero

The seven months they spent in London in 1797–98 were a happy time for Nelson's wife, for whom his affections seem to have been dwindling. He was forced to be dependent on her nursing, and on her unobtrusive help at numerous official dinners, when she would sit beside him and chop his food. Nelson was also highly popular with the people of London, as is evident from one particular incident which occurred during his stay at New Bond Street. One night, after a day of constant pain, Nelson retired to bed early in the hope of some respite. Southey tells us that the capital had just heard the news of Duncan's victory, and a jubilant mob came and knocked loudly at the door of the house, since unlike the rest it had not been illuminated in celebration. However, when they were told that Admiral Nelson lay in bed upstairs badly wounded, the crowd quietened, and their leader

103 New Bond Street,
Nelson's home 1797-98

replied 'You shall hear no more from us tonight': and 'the feeling
of respect and sympathy was communicated from one to another
with such effect, that, under the confusion of such a night, the
house was not molested again'.

Finally Nelson recovered fully, and was able to send a note to
the vicar of St George's, Hanover Square, saying that: 'An Officer
desires to return thanks to Almighty God for his perfect recovery
from a severe wound, and also for the many mercies bestowed
upon him.'

Early in 1798, Nelson rejoined the *Vanguard*, and sailed for
the Mediterranean at the request of an anxious Admiralty, to
divert the attention of Napoleon from his evident intention of
invading England. Nelson's arrival was decisive, as he effectively
cut off Napoleon's eastern army with a brilliant victory over the
French in Aboukir Bay, for which he was made a baron.

Emma Hamilton

1798 was also a momentous year for Nelson for another reason.
After Aboukir Bay he returned to Naples, where he re-encountered
Lady Emma Hamilton, the wife of the British Ambassador, a
meeting which was the beginning of a long and indiscreet affair.
By the time they reached London the following year, Nelson was
clearly enslaved, and though the populace at large still regarded
Nelson as a great hero, he was virtually ostracized by society as a
consequence of the affair and his callous treatment of his wife.
Over the following years he stayed in a variety of lodgings as near
to the Hamiltons as possible, until Emma procured for the
curious trio a 'farm', Merton Place near Wimbledon, where
Nelson could entertain in style with Emma as his hostess, while
Sir William Hamilton looked on. The latter died in 1803, but
Nelson and Emma's idyll was short-lived, as Nelson met his
death on 21 October 1805 at Trafalgar.

Sir Isaac Newton (1642–1727)

87 Jermyn Street, SW1

Newton was not happy when he first came to stay in London in 1689: he complained of 'confinement to the London air and to such a way of living as I am not in love with'. He returned from London, where he had been acting as Member of Parliament for Cambridge University, with few regrets, and resumed his activities as Lucasian Professor at Cambridge. Of a retiring and somewhat puritanical nature, he seems to have preferred by far the peaceful isolation of that university city. But he returned to London in 1696, taking up lodgings in Jermyn Street, and interestingly enough seems to have plunged himself eagerly into a new kind of life.

By 1696, the bulk of what were regarded both then and now as Newton's great scientific achievements — his discoveries about the nature of light and gravity — were behind him, the *Principia Mathematica* having been published in 1687. After that date he devoted himself to his increasing interest in theology, chronology, and alchemy, isolating himself from the Royal Society, especially after quarrelling with its leading light Robert Hooke. In 1693 he seems to have suffered a psychological breakdown of some kind, and to help him his friends John Locke and Charles Montague (later Earl of Halifax) procured for him the position of Master of the Mint.

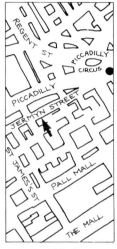

Tube: Piccadilly Circus.
Bus: Nos. 3, 6, 9, 12, 13, 15, 19, 22, 38, 53, 88, 159.

Jermyn Street

As this entailed moving to London, Newton first occupied quarters in the Tower of London, before, in 1697, becoming a tenant in Jermyn Street, where he spent the next thirteen years: he probably lived for a few years at no. 88 before moving to no. 87. It seems likely that no. 87, on which the blue plaque has been erected, is substantially the building it was in Newton's time, though the frontage has been seriously altered since then.

Jermyn Street was part of a very recent fashionable development on what had until the late 1660s been a field, known as St James's Field. This development was in fact inspired by Charles II, and set in motion by Henry Jermyn, Earl of St Albans, who had the idea of creating an estate of houses for aristocrats built around a central square — a novel idea at the time. By obtaining a

The doorway at 87 Jermyn Street

leasehold from the King and by letting out plots to speculative builders, he created St James's Square and several new roads around it, which were given such predictable titles as King Street, Charles II Street, Duke Street, and of course Jermyn Street. Most aristocrats at the time actually chose to live close by in Pall Mall (also built for Charles II) rather than in the new development, but among Newton's neighbours in Jermyn Street were Halifax and St Albans himself.

Although the position Newton had been given was considered by many, including some of his predecessors, to be a sinecure — Newton had been told that it had 'not too much business to require more attendance than you can spare' — he took his duties very seriously indeed. Newton ran the Mint with great energy, presiding over many criminal hearings as well as carrying out the complicated and mammoth task of the recoinage of the realm. He became so involved that in 1699 he resigned his fellowship and professorship at Cambridge. He also became increasingly involved with the Royal Society, taking over as its President from 1703, and he established himself as indisputably the king of science in his famous and victorious quarrels with the Royal Astronomer Flamsteed and with Leibniz. By saving the Royal Society from bankruptcy and introducing strict procedure to its meetings, Newton's practical genius also helped to forestall the satirical criticisms of what scoffers called the 'unfit entertainment' of its meetings. He was awarded a knighthood by Queen Anne in 1705.

In London

Indeed, Newton's whole existence was drastically altered by his move to London. The company into which he was thrown by his appointment, who no doubt resembled the cast of John Gay's *Beggar's Opera*, must initially have come as a shock to a man who was used to the refined manners of Cambridge and who had once dismissed a man from his presence for telling a joke about a nun! Yet Newton seems to have had no objection to a liaison between his niece Catherine Barton, who lived in his houses in London for over twenty years, and the Earl of Halifax. The laxity of society in the early eighteenth century, and perhaps his own mellowing, certainly modified Newton's outward conduct — he was now often to be seen in coffee houses after meetings of the Royal Society, appeared at Court, and even once recorded his attendance at an opera, which he apparently left halfway through on the grounds that it was 'too much of a good thing'. He seems to have grown somewhat corpulent, being frequently carried around town in a sedan chair. Of his home life we know very little, though he apparently lived well, with six servants, and was thought most hospitable by guests. His niece's recorded impressions of him portray Newton as the typical absent-minded scientist: he 'would let his dinner stand on the table two hours; his gruel, or milk and eggs that was carried to him warm for supper, wd eat cold for breakfast'.

Eventually, in 1710, Newton moved from Jermyn Street to St Martin's Street, Leicester Fields, and then again to Kensington in 1724. This latter move was for health reasons: his niece's husband, John Conduitt, tells us that he suffered in old age from, among other ailments, the 'disease of the stone', and was persuaded to move to the more rural surroundings of Kensington in January 1724, 'After which he was visibly better than he had been for some years'. But it is interesting to record that, in contrast to the feelings he had had about London in 1689, he now could not be kept away, as Conduitt tells us: '. . . though he found the greatest benefit from rest, and the air at Kensington, and was always worse for leaving it, no methods that were used could keep him from coming sometimes to town.' He died on 20 March 1727, only a few days after presiding over a meeting of the Royal Society, and was buried in Westminster Abbey.

Samuel Pepys (1633–1703)

12 Buckingham Street, WC2

Tube: Charing Cross.
Bus: Nos. 1, 6, 9, 11, 13, 15, 77, 168, 170, 172, 176.

Samuel Pepys lived in London all his life, and is of course best known as the diarist of the 1660s who chronicled the Great Fire and the Plague years. In 1679, when he came to live in Buckingham Street, he had, however, been subject to another somewhat harrowing experience — imprisonment in the Tower of London.

In the Tower

Pepys was one of many who did not escape from the hysteria surrounding the 'Popish Plot' of 1679. As an important figure in the Admiralty, once married to a Catholic who had converted just before her death in 1669, and a close associate of the Duke of York who also became a Catholic in 1672, Pepys was an obvious suspect in the alleged plot to put a Catholic king on the throne, and was arrested in 1678 on trumped-up charges and put in a cell in the Tower. But his friends stood by him, and after six weeks he was released on bail. Fortunately he was able to find refuge early in 1679 with William Hewer, his former clerk and oldest friend, at the latter's house, 12 Buckingham Street, where he received from Hewer 'all the care, kindness and faithfulness of a son'. Here Pepys devoted much of his time and energy to clearing his name,

An engraving of the Tower of London. *(Reproduced by kind permission of Robert Douwma Prints & Maps Ltd, London)*

12 Buckingham Street

until he was discharged in June 1680.

The Duke of Buckingham

The area to which he had moved was a fashionable new development, closely associated with the name of Buckingham. The
Duke of Buckingham, who had occupied York Place which
previously dominated the area, had moved to the City to dramatize
his quarrel with the Court, and in the 1670s sold the house to one
of London's most notorious developers, Nicholas Barbon. York
Place, one of Westminster's famous palaces, was promptly
demolished, and in its place quickly grew up an ambitious
complex of streets of a kind which were changing the face of
London dramatically in the late seventeenth century. The Duke
of Buckingham, anxious to be remembered in the Strand, insisted
that not only his title but his Christian and family names should
all be commemorated in the new streets: so the streets were duly
named George Street, Villiers Street, Duke Street, Buckingham
Street and even Of Alley (now ponderously entitled 'York Place,
formerly known as Of Alley'). This penchant for personal street
names was rivalled a century later when the Adam brothers
redeveloped the area, and happily named all the streets after
themselves.

All that now remains of York Place, once the palace of the
Archbishops of York, is York Watergate at the foot of the street,
which once marked the northern bank of the Thames, now

separated from the river by the Embankment Gardens.

Though it is now much altered, 12 Buckingham Street was clearly a very pleasant new house, with six bays. It was conveniently close to the river for transport, and also to the New Exchange in the Strand, a seventeenth-century 'shopping centre': designed by Simon Basil, Robert Cecil's Officer of Works, it had been opened by James I in 1609, and contained over one hundred shops on its ground and upper floors. It was particularly fashionable after the Fire had destroyed many of the shops in the City, and Pepys was no doubt often to be seen in one of the many excellent book shops on the ground floor. Though the area became less fashionable during the eighteenth century, Buckingham Street continued to attract a number of famous residents, including Robert Harley, Peter the Great, Henry Fielding, Jean-Jacques Rousseau, David Hume and Peg Woffington.

Back in power

Although Pepys' career in the Admiralty had suffered a severe setback in 1678, it was becoming clear that the Navy was incompetently run without him, and when he returned in 1684 from a successful expedition to destroy the fortifications at Tangier, he was rewarded with his old post of Secretary to the Admiralty. Shortly afterwards, there was a highly dramatic fire in the street when the wooden waterworks by the river caught fire; to prevent it from spreading, nos. 13 and 14 had to be blown up. Pepys watched from a safe vantage point, but many of his belongings were stolen from no. 12 in the confusion. However, undeterred, Pepys moved the Admiralty Office from Derby House to 12 Buckingham Street in September 1684, and later, when nos. 13 and 14 were rebuilt in 1688, transferred to no. 14. (So closely were York Buildings, as this row of houses had become known, associated with the Admiralty, that there was much wrangling after Pepys' death as to who rightfully owned the house.)

Pepys was again under suspicion in 1689, which was to be expected given his loyalty to James II during the Revolution, and his attempt to muster England's naval forces in defence of James against William of Orange. Though he was soon released from imprisonment without being charged because of his ill health, at one stage, fearful of the continuing suspicion, he shut himself up in York Buildings for three months and related:

> my constant poreing, and sitting so long still in one
> posture, without any divertings or exercize, haveing for
> about a month past brought a humour down into one of
> my leggs, not only to the swelling it to allmost the size of
> both, but with the giving mee mighty pains, and disabling
> mee to this day to putt a shooe on that foot.

Pepys library

He now went into retirement and at 14 Buckingham Street
devoted his time to more literary pursuits. In the 1690s the house
became something of a salon, the centre of intellectual life in the
capital, where the 'Saturday Academists', a small group of
Fellows of the Royal Society (of which Pepys had been made
President in 1685), met every week. They met in Pepys' library,
where he had built up a vast and varied collection of literature. He
set himself a target of three thousand volumes, and even des-
patched his nephew on a tour of Europe to procure for him the
volumes he wanted. The library, and three volume catalogue,
were completed in 1701 (the library was bequeathed to Magdalene
College, Cambridge). In that year, Pepys moved to Hewer's
house in Clapham, mainly to help his failing health, and there
spent the two remaining years of his life.

The library of Samuel
Pepys' house in
Buckingham Street,
c. 1690. *(By permission,
Master and Fellows,
Magdalene College,
Cambridge)*

William Pitt (the Younger) (1759–1806)

120 Baker Street, W1

Tube: Baker Street.
Bus: Nos. 1, 2, 13, 30, 74, 113, 159.

For most of his career, William Pitt was resident at a house in London that needs little introduction: 10 Downing Street.

The old block

Pitt's meteoric rise to the premiership owed much to his upbringing as well as to his own brilliance. His father, Pitt the Elder, decided that the boy should be tutored at home in Hayes, Kent, so that he could personally school the boy in the art of politics. The child quickly and obligingly developed a burning fascination for the subject, and joyfully exclaimed at the age of seven, when his father had been made Earl of Chatham, that he was glad he was not the eldest son, because he wanted to speak in the House of Commons, like his father. He entered Parliament in January 1781, and made his maiden speech on 26 February, so movingly that Edmund Burke exclaimed 'It is not a chip off the old block; it is the old block himself.'

Thereafter Pitt's rise to power was rapid. Confident of his worth, he rejected several offers of junior government posts, until at the age of twenty-three he accepted the office of Chancellor of the Exchequer under Shelburne in 1782. That government quickly fell to the combined forces of Charles James Fox and Lord North, but when the new government was defeated in November 1783 over the India Bill, Pitt accepted the King's request to form a new government, and so became Prime Minister at the age of twenty-five. Fox declared that the new administration would not last until January; but it lasted until 1801.

Pitt's time was not spent entirely at Downing Street. He had few close friends, but one of them was William Wilberforce, the reformer, who at the time was living in Wimbledon. This prompted Pitt to lease a small house on the north side of Putney Heath in August 1784, and there he was able to benefit from the country air without neglecting his state duties. Later, in 1785, he purchased a country estate, Holwood Hill, near Bromley, Kent.

Despite Fox's scathing comments about the 'schoolboy' Prime Minister, Pitt remained in office for seventeen years, until his resignation over the Catholic Emancipation Bill, having weathered the storms of the French Revolution. He then moved for a while to a small house in Park Place (no. 12), and from there in autumn 1802 moved to another small house, 14 York Place, Portman Square (now 120 Baker Street). He remained there until May 1804 when, on the failure of Addington, Pitt was summoned by George III to reconstruct the ministry. Pitt then returned to Downing Street.

Private life

Paradoxically, the man who wrought miracles with the nation's finances was quite inept when it came to managing his own. The purchase of Holwood Hall had put him in dire straits, as he was extremely careless with his money. By 1802, his debts totalled

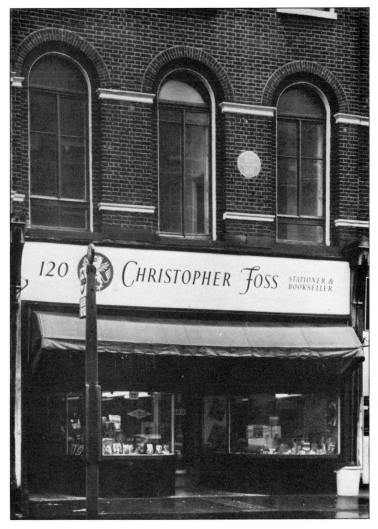

120 Baker Street

120 Baker Street as it was before the addition of a shop front

£45,000, and now that he was no longer in power his creditors became increasingly persistent: 'His houses were in danger of being stripped of their furniture, and his stables of their horses.' In 1803 he was forced to sell Holwood, and the move to York Place helped slightly, but his bills were still huge: for instance, the weekly food accounts still in existence from the residence at York Place show a meat consumption of half a ton a week! To add to the problem, Pitt's staff were probably defrauding him, as he was unable to afford a reliable steward to administer his domestic affairs.

As Lord Stanhope commented in his *Life of Pitt*,

> Accustomed as Pitt was to Downing Street and Whitehall, he must have felt some economy indeed, but considerable inconvenience, in a situation so far removed from the House of Commons.

The house in Baker Street, built c. 1790, was part of the Portman Estate which was growing rapidly during the late eighteenth century; Baker Street's name is derived from Sir Edward Baker, who helped Mr Portman develop the estate. At that time, this was a quiet outlying area, though in 1757 the New Road (now Marylebone Road) had been built as a bypass to the Oxford Road; this had the advantage of making areas like this much safer for travelling at night. Estates were also being developed further north at this time, such as the Eyre Estate in St John's Wood. Pitt's house is now not much altered, apart from the addition of a shop front.

A lively niece

The house was considerably enlivened by the residence there of Pitt's eccentric niece, Hester Stanhope, who later in life took up a somewhat different residence on Mount Lebanon in Syria. Lord Stanhope commented that 'her presence proved to be, as it were, the light in his dwelling ... and tended ... far more than his return to power to cheer and brighten his few ... remaining years'. She also frequently accompanied him on his visits to Walmer Castle in Kent, where he rode and sailed, and where he carried out his duties as Lord Warden of the Cinque Ports, supervising the coastal defences.

Pitt did not long survive his return to Downing Street: the burdens placed upon him, as Lady Hester Stanhope commented, were 'enough to kill a man ... it was murder'. The news of defeat at Austerlitz did little to restore the sick man, and returning from Bath in January 1806 to Bowling Green House in Putney, which he had leased eighteen months earlier, Pitt died in the early hours of 23 January, the twenty-fifth anniversary of his entry into Parliament.

Robert Falcon Scott (1868–1912)

56 Oakley Street, SW3

Robert Falcon Scott returned to London after his first Antarctic expedition in 1904 to find himself suddenly famous. The voyage of the *Discovery*, of which he was in command, had been a success: Scott had proved himself not only a resourceful leader but also a useful scientific investigator for the Royal Geographical Society, and for his services he was made a captain and given six months' leave to write up his survey of the South Victoria Sound.

Scott responded well to the turnabout in his fortunes. Fatherless, he lived with his mother and sisters in London, supporting them as best he could. Now, with the pay which had accumulated during his voyage, he was able to meet these burdens, enabling his mother and sisters to move from lodgings into their own house, 56 Oakley Street in Chelsea, just off the Embankment. Though the area was cheap and unfashionable, the Scotts were happy with their new residence, a pleasant house built in the 1850s, and it remained their home for four years.

Tube: Sloane Square or South Kensington.
Bus: Nos. 11, 19, 22, 39, 49.

In demand

Scott was soon in demand to give lectures on his adventures, and the quietly modest naval officer was well received by his audiences, which varied from eminent scientists to young children. One correspondent reported:

> He hardly used any long words. He talked of scientific observations as though they were a new game, and of hardships and dangers as though they were the best fun in the world.

An exhibition of his photographs taken on the voyage together with Edward Wilson's drawings opened in November 1904, and attracted much public attention, reflecting the enormous interest which the voyage had inspired.

Much of Scott's time in 1905 was taken up with writing his book, *The Voyage of the Discovery*, which was probably written partly at Oakley Street. He was uncertain of the book's worth:

> I have tied myself to a desk. . . . The resultant book will be very dull but it will not outstrip fact and I'm really rather indifferent to profits though by rights I can't afford to be.

Above, left: the *Discovery,* now moored at St Katharine's Dock, E1; *right:* 56 Oakley Street

However, his doubts were unjustified, and when the book was published in October it was warmly received by the critics, who admired the writer's self-effacing but vivid style.

It was while he was living at Oakley Street that Scott, home on a short leave from his ship the *Albermarle,* met his future wife, the sculptress Kathleen Bruce, a highly unconventional woman who, after living alone in Paris for some years had recently settled in London and was now living in Cheyne Walk, near Scott's own house. Since his famous voyage, Scott had been popular with many London hostesses as an eligible if not young bachelor, and it was at a tea party given by Mabel Beardsley (the sister of the artist) that the seemingly unsuited couple met. Within a month, however, in the knowledge that Scott's leave would soon expire, they were engaged to be married. Scott's major worry was their mutual impecunity, but he was partly relieved of his domestic burdens when, early in 1908, 56 Oakley Street was given up, his mother having decided to go to live in Henley on Thames. In Scott's absence, Kathleen found a suitably modest marital home at 174 Buckingham Palace Road (since demolished), and furnished it 'from auction sales in poky places in Pimlico'. The couple were married in September 1908, less than a year after their first meeting.

Their happiness was to be short-lived: Scott was already making plans for a second Antarctic expedition and, although delayed by Shackleton's intervening attempt to reach the South Pole, Scott's expedition eventually set sail in June 1910. He was never to return from the ill-fated journey: delayed by fierce blizzards and low temperatures, Scott and his companions arrived at the Pole in January 1912 to find they had been beaten by Amundsen, and all died on the journey back to base.

George Bernard Shaw (1856–1950)

29 Fitzroy Square, W1

In 1876, at the age of twenty, George Bernard Shaw moved from Dublin to his mother's house in Fulham, 13 Victoria Grove (now Netherton Grove). In 1882, the family moved to lodgings at 36 Osnaburgh Street, St Pancras, where they remained for five years, until they took rooms in the more fashionable West End, at no. 29 Fitzroy Square.

Blissful unemployment

Before coming to London, Shaw had worked for five years as a clerk for a Dublin estate agent. Now in London, he remained blissfully unemployed for many years, living off his mother. He came to England quite determined to be a novelist, but in the eleven years before the move to Fitzroy Square, publishers displayed a singular lack of interest in his efforts. But Shaw was nothing if not determined — he described his method of novel-writing thus:

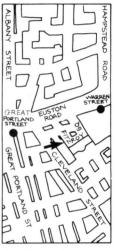

Tube: Warren Street.
Bus: Nos. 14, 18, 24, 27, 29, 30, 73, 134, 176.

> I bought supplies of white paper, demy size, by sixpennorths at a time; folded it in quarto; and condemned myself to fill five pages of it a day, rain or shine, dull or inspired. I had so much of the schoolboy and the clerk still in me that if my five pages ended in the middle of a sentence I did not finish it until next day. On the other hand, if I missed a day, I made up for it by doing a double task on the morrow. On this plan I produced five novels in five years.

However, seeking alternative employment was far from Shaw's mind, and apart from 'ghosting' some music criticism, his only employment was a brief stint in 1879 with the Edison Telephone Company. His painful shyness was not an asset in this occupation:

> I presently found myself studying the topography of the east end of London, and trying to persuade all sorts of people to allow the Company to put insulators and poles and derricks and the like on their roofs to carry the telephone lines. I liked the exploration involved; but my shyness made the business of calling on strangers frightfully

29 Fitzroy Square, later also the home of Virginia Stephen

uncongenial; and my sensitiveness, which was extreme... made the impatient rebuffs I had to endure occasionally, especially from much worried women who mistook me for an advertisement canvasser, ridiculously painful to me.

Musical ability

Some sort of breakthrough came in 1885, when William Archer, whom Shaw had met in the British Museum while reading Marx, invited him to become art critic for the *World*. Loath to take on regular employment, Shaw nevertheless accepted, and from there graduated to the post of music critic of the *Star* and then of the *World*. His own musical ability, however, hardly qualified him for the task in hand — in an effort to emulate the successful musicians in his family (his mother was a piano teacher) he would frequently make painful attempts to bash through the scores of the great classics on the piano, causing anguish to the other inhabitants of Fitzroy Square as well as to his mother:

I used to drive her nearly crazy by my favourite selections from Wagner's Ring, which to her was 'all recitative' and horribly discordant at that. She never complained at the time, but confessed it after we separated, and said that she had sometimes gone away to cry....

Success

Music criticism was left behind when in 1895 Shaw achieved a major success by becoming dramatic critic of Frank Harris's *Saturday Review*. He had, by this time, discovered his métier as a dramatist rather than a novelist; and while at Fitzroy Square wrote many of his plays, including *The Philanderer* and *Mrs Warren's Profession* (1893), and *Arms and the Man* and *Candida* (1894). Though considered unactable at the time as well as too daring in content, the plays were soon to be performed to packed houses.

During this period also Shaw became increasingly active politically: having for some years been a member of the Fabian Society, in 1897 he became a member of the St Pancras Parish Council, serving until 1903. The area was one of the most deprived in London, and as Shaw wrote:

> It was cheerfully corrupt politically: a cheque for £1,000, placed in the right quarter, would have secured the return of a baby in arms to Parliament or the County Council for the southern division, where I resided.

An active campaigner for better conditions for the poor, Shaw was particularly determined in his attempts to obtain better services for women, which at the time seemed a demand so outrageous that he was considered a crank, and was why,

> when on that public body I talked and talked to get proper, common, sanitary accommodation for women, I found it impossible for a long time to get over the opposition to it as an indecency. A lavatory for women was described as an abomination.

In 1898, Shaw married an Irish millionairess, Charlotte Payne-Townshend, and left Fitzroy Square for a house in the country. He now lived permanently in the country, although from 1899 he had a London *pied-à-terre* at 10 Adelphi Terrace. The Shaws' home in Ayot St Lawrence, Hertfordshire, where Shaw died at the age of ninety-four, is now a Shaw museum.

Of Shaw's London addresses, both 13 Victoria Grove and 36 Osnaburgh Street have been demolished and are, respectively, the sites of a nurses' home and an office block. Fortunately 29 Fitzroy Square (which was also the home of Virginia Stephen from 1907–11), part of a stuccoed terrace built 1827–35, still stands, little altered externally since the 1880s.

Ellen Terry (1847–1928)

22 Barkston Gardens, SW5

Tube: Earls Court.
Bus: Nos. 30, 31, 74.

It was not until 1889, when she was forty-two, that Ellen Terry moved with her two children to 22 Barkston Gardens, in a quiet part of Chelsea. It was an area which she knew well, since through her early (and disastrous) marriage to the painter G.F. Watts and her association with the architect E.W. Godwin (with whom she lived from 1868 until 1875, and who was the father of her children), she knew many of the Chelsea artists and writers — Rossetti, Whistler, Sickert, and Wilde.

A working house

Despite her success and prestige, Ellen Terry's new house was to be a family home above all else, and not a *salon*, as her son Gordon wrote: 'Ours was not planned as a sociable house, or a society house — it was a working house.' It was strewn with comfortable chairs, there were two pianos in the parlour, and the whole house was festooned with window boxes. Ellen's rooms occupied the whole second floor, with a bedroom at the front and a large dressing room at the back.

The period during which Ellen lived at Barkston Gardens saw the continuation of her great partnership at the Lyceum Theatre with Henry Irving, which had begun in 1878. Irving had made Ellen a national figure of greater stature than any previous actress in London, and Ellen's Shakespearian roles never failed to pull in the crowds. However, the 1890s were in some ways a period of sadness for her, as Irving had formed a new friendship with Mrs Eliza Aria, and no longer needed Ellen's emotional support. Furthermore, though Ellen and Irving continued to act together at the Lyceum, their traditional brand of theatre was going out of fashion, and Irving was increasingly criticized for his continued espousal of Shakespeare and neglect of the new drama. In 1899 a syndicate took over the management of the theatre from Irving, but it continued to lose money.

The famous painting of Ellen Terry by her first husband G.F. Watts

Strange friendship

There were consolations for Ellen: her famous friendship with George Bernard Shaw, ironically the most scathing of the new

22 Barkston Gardens, now
a hotel

generation of drama critics, coincided with her stay at Barkston
Gardens. They first came into contact when Ellen Terry wrote
to Shaw in his capacity as a music critic to give her an opinion
on a young friend who was a singer; from then on they continued
to correspond, agreeing for a long time never to meet. The
strange friendship helped to sustain Ellen and direct her talents
towards the new drama — she had considerable success in
several of Shaw's plays.

Ellen Terry left Barkston Gardens in 1902, the same year
that the Lyceum, still losing money, closed down. In 1904 Ellen
moved to 215 King's Road, Chelsea, where she stayed until
1920, largely in retirement. That house, built in 1720, is still
standing, as is 22 Barkston Gardens, which remains much as
it was in the 1890s. The theatre with which Ellen Terry was so
strongly associated, on Wellington Street, WC2, is still in
existence; however, it was almost entirely rebuilt in 1902–4, and
only the back wall and the portico remain of the theatre where
she and Henry Irving acted together.

J.M.W. Turner (1775–1851)

40 Sandycoombe Road, Twickenham and 119 Cheyne Walk, SW10

Sandycoombe Road:
Rail: St Margarets
(overground from
Waterloo).
Bus: Nos. 27, 33, 37, 73, 90,
90B, 202, 270.

In 1810, Turner was at the height of his success as an artist. Though a rather surly, sensitive man with a reputation for pride and tactlessness, his genius as a landscape painter was widely recognized, and in 1809 he had been made Professor of Perspective at the Royal Academy. Contrary to the popular image of the artist shivering in a garret, he was relatively wealthy: so at the age of thirty-four he was able to buy a long strip of land in Twickenham, and proceed to build himself a house as an additional residence to his home in the West End, 23 Queen Anne Street, Cavendish Square (now demolished).

In his youth Turner had studied to be an architect, and in old age is reputed to have said, 'If I could have my time over again, I would be an architect.' He thus designed the new house himself: his sketch books contain many drawings and plans of Sandycombe Lodge, while he also personally supervised the construction of the house, which was completed early in 1813. The finished house, little altered today, was Italianate in style; it was designed around a central block, where he had his studio, which had a large, long window to catch the morning light. The central block is one window wide, with two storeys and a basement, and an entrance porch surmounted by a first floor balcony. The two small wings were originally single-storeyed, but were later built upon.

The setting was extremely picturesque. As well as overseeing the design of the house, Turner also made improvements to the garden, which sloped gently down to the east of the house, by enlarging the existing pond, in which he grew waterplants to introduce into the foregrounds of his pictures. He planted the garden thickly with willows so that, as his friend Trimmer recorded, he could 'refresh his eye with the run of the boughs from his sitting-room window'.

A fashionable neighbourhood

The village of Twickenham was pleasant and fashionable, popular at the time with writers and artists. From the upper window of Sandycombe Lodge there was a fine view across the Thames to Richmond Hill, where Sir Joshua Reynolds had lived, while one

40 Sandycoombe Road, Twickenham, the house designed by Turner himself

of Turner's most discerning patrons, the Duke of Northumberland, was a close neighbour at Syon House. The area indeed inspired several of Turner's works, including the view of Richmond Hill on the Prince Regent's birthday, one of Turner's largest paintings (now in the Tate Gallery).

Though Turner seems at first to have intended the house at Twickenham to be a permanent retreat in which he could paint undisturbed (he initially called the house Solus Lodge, as an indication of this), he seems to have quickly become a well known Twickenham resident, making various acquaintances, and inviting other Academists to visit him there. He was often seen around Twickenham, and was much respected, being a regular attender at church, though at the same time he was given the somewhat irreverent nickname of 'Overturner' by other locals, a reflection of the way he drove his horse and gig about the village. He became a close friend of Henry Scott Trimmer, the vicar of nearby Heston, and his son, and Turner, acutely aware of his lack of a classical education, gave Trimmer the elder painting lessons in exchange for a course in Latin and Greek, at which Turner proved to be singularly lacking in aptitude. Turner seems to have been much in love with Trimmer's daughter, but too shy to ask her to marry him. But he seems to have been happy at Sandycombe Lodge, where he could indulge in fishing, his favourite sport, and boating on the river Thames.

Return to the West End

However, Turner does not seem to have stayed at Twickenham for long: the indications are that he left the house in 1815 or 1816. The reason seems to have been partly that he was suffering from a temporary fall in income, as a result of adverse criticism of his work. Another reason was that his father, who lived with him, was perpetually catching colds, as the house was always chilly and caught little sun. Turner's father also had to travel up to the West End daily, either to mind the gallery of Turner's paintings at the Queen Anne Street house, or to dress the wigs of his old clients from his days as a barber in Maiden Lane, Covent Garden (where Turner had been born). The expense and time of the journey were not welcome to the old man, though he does seem eventually to have found a novel solution to the problem, as he related with some satisfaction to a friend:

> Why, lookee here, I have found a way at last of coming up cheap from Twickenham to open my son's gallery — I found out the inn where the market-gardeners baited their horses, I made friends with one on 'em, and now, for a glass of gin a day, he brings me up in his cart on the top of the vegetables.

So, for whatever reason, the Turners moved back to Queen Anne Street. It was Turner's home until 1851, and was somewhat neglected during his tenancy, having a 'blistered dirty house-door and black-crusted windows', while the first-floor gallery, where Turner hung the pictures which may now be seen in the National Gallery, was bare and chilly. Here Turner lived a solitary existence after his father's death in 1839.

Turner's secret residence

There is another, privately erected plaque to Turner, at 119 Cheyne Walk, Chelsea, which marks Turner's residence there during the last few years of his life. Always a secretive person, he suddenly stopped living at his house in Queen Anne Street, and for four years before his death, no one knew where he was living. Then, by chance, his housekeeper at Queen Anne Street, where he still appeared occasionally, found his address in a coat pocket, and it transpired that he was living, under the name of Booth, at Cremorne Cottage, 119 Cheyne Walk, Chelsea, with a lady of the

Tube: South Kensington.
Bus: Nos. 11, 19, 22, 39, 45, 49.

119 Cheyne Walk, where
Turner spent his last years

same name who had once been his housekeeper. Exactly when he
went to live there is unknown, but he seems to have painted a
large number of pictures at the house, using a second-floor room
as a studio, and often going up on to the railed roof to watch the
changing light of the skies at sunrise. A curious event occurred
some years after Turner's death concerning some of these
paintings. Apparently, John Ruskin discovered at the cottage a
room full of drawings and watercolours by Turner, none of which
had been catalogued. Greatly excited by the discovery, he applied
for and was granted permission to catalogue them. He then found
that among the paintings were a number of somewhat explicit life
studies of the mysterious Ms Booth. As he regarded these as
pornographic, he proceeded to burn them!

Though a project to make 119 Cheyne Walk into a Turner
Museum failed, the house, which dates from the late eighteenth
century, still stands, and has been enlarged by the addition of the
adjoining house, no. 118, a building of later date.

Mark Twain (Samuel Langhorne Clemens) (1835–1910)

23 Tedworth Square, SW3

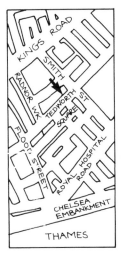

Tube: Sloane Square.
Bus: Nos. 11, 19, 22, 39, 45, 49.

Mark Twain's visit to London in 1896–97, when he was sixty-one, was made for slightly unusual reasons for a rich and successful author. Back in America, he had invested heavily in a publishing and typesetting venture, the Charles L. Webster Co. For a time the firm was spectacularly profitable; it then failed equally spectacularly, leaving Twain with immense debts.

Lecture tour

He therefore decided to embark on an extended lecture tour in order to raise enough money to pay off his debts — 'Apparently I've *got* to mount the lecture platform next fall or I'll starve' he lamented. Ever since Dickens had stormed America with his platform readings from his novels, such lecture tours had been greatly in vogue. Mark Twain's tour, which began in 1895, took him across the American continent, and thence to Australia, India, Ceylon and Africa. He finally docked in Southampton, which he regarded as the end of the tour, in July 1896. His task in England was to review his finances before returning to America.

On arriving in London after a stay in Guildford, Surrey, Mark Twain, his wife and two of their daughters moved into a large Victorian house in Chelsea — no. 23 Tedworth Square. They arrived here deeply saddened by the news which had reached them at Guildford that their other daughter, Susy, at home in America, had died of meningitis, at the age of twenty-four. The news made another reason for them to stay on in England for a while, so that they could be alone with their grief. The house in Chelsea was found for them by Mark Twain's publishers, and the Clemens family took up the tenancy in October, paying a rent of 5½ guineas a week.

The grief that the Clemenses felt at this time led them to shun all company except that of a few trusted friends. Twain's reticence led to a rumour being circulated to the effect that his family had deserted him and that, alone, sick and in poverty, he was labouring to repay his debts. However, a nephew, visiting 23 Tedworth Square, found him in good spirits, in comfortable

23 Tedworth Square

surroundings, and together with his family.

More Tramps Abroad

The need to come to terms with his bereavement impelled Mark
Twain into a new period of intensive writing. The book on which
he was engaged, issued in England as *More Tramps Abroad* and
in America as *Following the Equator*, was the only one of his
works to be written entirely in England (which he had visited on
several previous occasions). His last travel book, it was the
result of the lecture tour of 1895–96. He wrote of it in 1899:

> I wrote my last travel book in hell; but I let on, the best I
> could, that it was an excursion through heaven. Some day I
> will read it, & if its lying cheerfulness fools me, then I shall
> believe it fooled the reader. How I did loathe that journey
> round the world!

But, like the tour, and despite Twain's misgivings, the book
was successful, especially in its English sales, and in July 1896
the Clemenses were able to return home to America, with all
their debts paid.

Horace Walpole (1717–97)

5 Arlington Street, SW1
and Strawberry Hill, Waldegrave Road, Twickenham

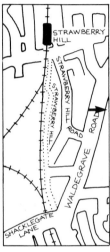

Strawberry Hill:
Rail: Strawberry Hill
(overground from
Waterloo).
Bus: Nos. 27, 270, 281.
Arlington Street:
Tube: Green Park.
Bus: Nos. 9, 14, 19, 22, 25,
38.

Even at the time when it was built, the villa which Horace Walpole built for himself at Twickenham was considered so extraordinary that Walpole felt obliged to issue tickets to visitors to control the crowds. For he had set out to build at Strawberry Hill no ordinary house, but a castle of Gothic splendour; and four architects were employed to transform the small cottage Walpole had bought in 1748 into an edifice unlike anything else in London — it was to be the product of Horace Walpole's imagination.

A Gothic castle

From the outside, Walpole's home still has the appearance of a miniature Gothic castle, with its turrets, battlements and lancet windows: to the original fabric of the house Walpole added a refectory, a library, cloisters and a round tower. Inside, the effect is even more fantastic: the entire 'castle' is embellished with Gothic fretwork, shields and ornaments, reaching a climax in the fan vaulted ceiling of the gallery, copied from the Henry VII chapel at Westminster Abbey. It was a fitting setting for Walpole's vast library of books, housed in flamboyant Gothic bookcases, and his valuable collection of works of art.

Content that his house was the talking point of London, Horace Walpole was happy to live a quiet and uneventful life. He derived a comfortable income from certain sinecures obtained for him by his father Robert, the Prime Minister; and was able to live the typical life of an eighteenth century gentleman dilettante. In 1757, he set up his own printing press in the grounds at Strawberry Hill, and over the next thirty years published a number of fine editions of the classics, in which his own interests lay, and also several of his own works on the visual arts, including *Anecdotes of Painting in England* (1762–71) and *A Catalogue of Engravers* (1763). Aside from keeping up a massive and varied correspondence, for which he is perhaps best known today, he also published a Gothic novel, *The Castle of Otranto* (1765) written, not surprisingly, at Strawberry Hill. This proved enormously popular, setting a new vogue for such novels, whose main ingredients were haunted Gothic castles, plenty of intrigue and passion, and brainless heroines, ridiculed delightfully by Jane

Austen in *Northanger Abbey*.

Horace Walpole divided his time between his pleasant country residence, a welcome contrast to his father's vast and draughty mansion at Houghton in Norfolk, and London. Until 1779 he lived when in London at his father's house in Arlington Street, spending some time also with his father at Downing Street; then in October 1779 he took possession of no. 11 Berkeley Square (now demolished: Berkeley Square House now stands on this site), and declared: 'I am well pleased with my new habitation as I can be with anything at present.' Here he was able to indulge in one of his favourite occupations, the observation of other people's

Strawberry Hill – no ordinary house! It is now part of St Mary's College; visits may be made by arrangement with the Principal's Secretary

The gallery at Strawberry Hill

behaviour, since Berkeley Square was already a highly fashionable residence. He died at this house on 2 March 1797.

Violence

However, life was not all serenity: indeed, Horace Walpole's voluminous correspondence gives us many glimpses of the violence of London life at the time, as Walpole had a habit of recording all the mishaps that befell him. On one occasion he had the alarming experience of being almost shot in Hyde Park by a highwayman, whose pistol exploded in his face — a reminder that although carriages usually traversed Hyde Park in armed convoy, highway robberies were still frequent. Poor Walpole complained that one was 'forced to travel even at noon as if one was going into battle ... what a shambles this country is grown!'. Even at Twickenham, then London's most fashionable suburb, he felt threatened, declaring that none of his neighbours felt safe even at home; a view rather alarmingly strengthened when Walpole rushed to Berkeley Square from Strawberry Hill on hearing that his footman at Berkeley Square had pawned his silver strainer and spoons, only to find that the unfortunate thief had fled to Strawberry Hill, and hanged himself from a tree in the garden. To crown it all, there was a gunpowder manufacturer nearby at North Feltham, and the explosions which occurred there every few months terrified the local populace, including Walpole, who complained that Strawberry Hill was once damaged by an explosion. It seemed that he was not safe anywhere.

5 Arlington Street, where Horace Walpole lived for some years with his father

Arthur Wellesley, Duke of Wellington (1769–1852)

Apsley House (Wellington Museum), 149 Piccadilly, W1

Apsley House, or 'Number 1 London' as it has been known since the early nineteenth century, was first bought by the Duke of Wellington in 1817, and the crown freehold was presented to him in 1830, in gratitude for his services to the nation. It was a fitting tribute to a man whose military career had ended gloriously at Waterloo on 18 June 1815 when the French were routed by the English and Prussian armies.

The Duke of Wellington bought the house from his brother, the 1st Marquess Wellesley, in 1817. Originally designed by Robert Adam, the house was built between 1771 and 1778 for the second Earl Bathurst. The Adam house was in red brick (Adam's plans are preserved in Sir John Soane's Museum, Lincoln's Inn Fields) but during the Duke of Wellington's time the house was faced in Bath stone, giving it its present appearance, and extended by the addition of a Corinthian portico and the western Waterloo Gallery wing.

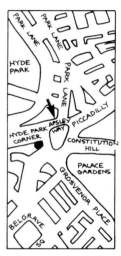

Tube: Hyde Park Corner.
Bus: Nos. 2, 9, 14, 16, 19, 22, 25, 30, 36, 38, 52, 73, 74, 137, 500.

Apsley House, known as 'No. 1 London', probably because for many years it was the first house in London encountered by travellers from the West. Now the Wellington Museum, it is open to the public throughout the year Tue-Thu and Sat 10.00-18.00, and Sun 14.30-18.00. (Tel. 01-499 5676)

The improvements carried out by the architect Benjamin Dean Wyatt at the Duke of Wellington's instigation were extensive. Like other contemporary great houses, such as Buckingham Palace and Clarence House, Apsley House was sumptuously redecorated in the opulent Louis XIV style then in fashion, and this is the style in which the museum is preserved today, though Robert Adam's fine barrel-vaulted ceiling may still be admired in the Piccadilly Drawing Room. Most of the paintings now on display were collected by the Duke, and some have a curious history. They were given to the Duke after they had been captured at the Battle of Vittoria in Spain in 1813 from Joseph Bonaparte, who had taken them from the Spanish Royal Collections. Somewhat embarassed by these circumstances, the Duke wrote to the King of Spain after Bonaparte's expulsion, offering their return; but nobly the King, regarding the paintings as rightful 'spoils of war', refused to deprive the Duke of his prized collection. Another curious, and famous, exhibit at Apsley House is the gigantic naked statue of Napoleon by Canova bought by the Duke, who no doubt appreciated the fact that Napoleon himself, for whom the statue was made, absolutely hated it!

Politics

Shortly after settling in to Apsley House the Duke, his military career over, went into politics, taking a seat in the Cabinet, from which he resigned in 1827 over a disagreement with Canning. On the latter's death he was invited back, and made Prime Minister. His brief administration saw the repeal of the Test and Corporation Acts in 1828 and the Catholic Emancipation Act in 1829. However, particularly over the issue of parliamentary reform, which many in Parliament were claiming was desperately overdue since disaffection in the country was rife, Wellington proved to be a classic example of a military man turned politician: success at the former occupation was in his case almost a guarantee of failure at the other. Indiscreet by conviction, his brusque tactics did not work in Parliament. He succeeded, at a stroke, in alienating any following he might have had by making a peculiarly insensitive speech in Parliament in 1830 to the effect that he believed the present parliamentary representation could in no way be rendered more satisfactory. When he sat down, there was quite a stir. Apparently, Wellington turned to Lord Aberdeen and whispered, 'What can I have said which seems to make so great a disturbance?' 'You have announced the fall of your government: that is all' came the reply. It was true: the government fell, making way for the Whigs to introduce sweeping parliamentary reforms. Wellington returned to power briefly as Foreign Secretary in 1834.

Wellington, c. 1827

An affair of honour

While at Apsley House, Wellington fought the only duel of his life. This stemmed from the Catholic Emancipation Act: the Act alienated a large part of Wellington's following in Parliament, and eventually Wellington challenged Lord Winchilsea to a duel, as the latter gentleman had insinuated that Wellington's motives for passing the Act were dishonourable. The duel took place in Battersea Fields (now Battersea Park), south of the river Thames, at dawn on 21 March 1829. It was entirely an affair of honour: the Duke intended to fire at Winchilsea's legs, but when he saw that Winchilsea's right arm remained fast by his side, he fired wide, and Winchilsea fired happily into the air, apologised, and honour was settled.

But the reaction to the Prime Minister's putting his life at risk was dismay, though the Duke himself was unconcerned: arriving afterwards at the home of his close friend, Mrs Arbuthnot, for breakfast, he enquired breezily 'Well, what do you think of a gentleman who has been fighting a duel?' 'I was amazed yesterday morning' wrote the lady later 'by the Duke walking in while I was at breakfast and telling me he had been fighting Lord Winchilsea ... The Duke went afterwards to Windsor and saw the King, who thought he was quite right.'

During the Reform crisis Wellington was even more unpopular. At the time when his wife Kitty lay dying in Apsley House, a mob came and smashed the windows, scattering immense quantities

Wellington's duel with Winchilsea in 1829 quickly became a popular subject for cartoonists, always eager to caricature the Duke. *(Reproduced by kind permission of Robert Douwma Prints & Maps Ltd, London)*

THE FIELD OF BATTERSEA

The bronze equestrian
statue of Wellington
which now stands on
Hyde Park Corner
opposite Apsley House

of new plate-glass everywhere. 'The people are gone mad' declared the Duke to Mrs Arbuthnot. He installed iron shutters on all the windows, and they remained there until his death.

Adulation

But he need not have worried, since his period of unpopularity was brief. Countless streets, institutions, towns, ships as well as boots were named after him and his victory at Waterloo, while statues of the Duke were erected in abundance: he was still remembered as the nation's military hero. Near Apsley House itself today are the Achilles statue, commemorating Wellington's victories, and an equestrian statue in bronze. Originally, one such statue topped the Constitution Hill arch, which now stands at an angle to the house, but which originally stood directly in front of it. Naturally this and the statue of Wellington topping it, together standing 100 feet high, cast a mighty shadow on Wellington's front windows at certain times of day. Despite this, Wellington was highly indignant when a proposal was mooted in the summer of 1846 to remove the statue, on the grounds that it looked totally ridiculous as a complement to Decimus Burton's triumphal arch, which had been designed to carry a four-horse chariot; one wag suggested that the statue would best belong on the bed of the Serpentine. Diplomatically, Queen Victoria vetoed the proposal, so as not to appear to humiliate the Duke in public, and not until thirty years after his death was the controversial statue removed to Aldershot, and a four-horse chariot at last put in its place.

The Duke's popularity reached its heights in 1851, when he was nearly mobbed by an adulatory crowd on one of his many visits to the Great Exhibition. After his death at Walmer Castle, Kent on 14 September 1852 a mammoth funeral took place, thought to be the grandest ever held in this country; over one and a half million people lined the route of the funeral procession past Apsley House to St Paul's Cathedral.

Wellington Museum

Since 1952, after the 7th Duke of Wellington presented his house to the nation, it has been open to the public as the Wellington Museum, although, in fact, from 1853 the public were allowed by the 2nd Duke to view the main apartments by appointment. The house is fortunate to have survived demolition schemes which were at one stage part of plans to ease traffic congestion at Hyde Park Corner. Happily, in 1961-62, Apsley House was separated from the original row of houses adjoining it called Piccadilly Terrace, which was demolished: Apsley House now stands on an island, in the midst of the frenzied traffic.

H.G. Wells (1866–1946)

13 Hanover Terrace, NW1

On 21 September 1866, Herbert George Wells was born unromantically over a hardware shop in Bromley High Street. The address, in what was then a separate community soon to become a suburb, had little to recommend it, and indeed Wells' vivid description of the process of suburbanization of 'Bromstead' in *The New Machiavelli* (1911) indicated his adverse feelings about such a place.

Grand design

Wells' last residence in London, to which a plaque has been affixed, could hardly have been in greater contrast. No. 13 Hanover Terrace is part of one of the superbly elegant terraces constructed by Nash as part of his grand design for Regent's Park. When this area of land became Crown Property in 1809, the Prince Regent expressed his desire for Nash to link architecturally his new palace at Carlton House with this area of open land to the north of Portland Place. Though Nash's grand plan — for terraces surrounding the park, many villas, small and large, scattered through it, and a large serpentine lake fed by a canal — was not fully realized, enough of it was built to give an impression of the breathtaking audacity of the scheme. The terraces around the park successfully created the illusion intended by Nash, for city residents to feel that they were living in palatial mansions, looking out on to vast grounds. Hanover Terrace is one of these, situated to the west of the park, a relatively short terrace built in 1822–23.

When Wells moved into the terrace in 1936, he took a fiendish delight in changing the number — 12a — to 13, which he put up in huge figures, and even enlarged during the War. His description of 13 Hanover Terrace as 'an old tumble-down house on the borders of Regent's Park', was hardly accurate; in fact, unlike at his previous residences, here Wells made an effort to furnish and decorate the rooms in style, and his friend Beatrice Webb commented that the house was 'attractive and luxuriously fitted'.

From here, despite his advanced years, Wells set off on a number of lecture tours of the United States and Australia, and

Tube: Baker Street or Marylebone.
Bus: Nos. 2, 2B, 13, 74, 113.

also continued to write feverishly. He was still writing novels though he had become more inclined towards non-fiction, and *The Shape of Things to Come* (1933) was followed by *Star Begotten* (1937). He also wrote two film screenplays, *Things to Come* and *Man Who Could Work Miracles*. However, with the impending war which he had prophesied so many years earlier, he wrote numerous articles and pamphlets on the subject, while in *The Fate of Homo Sapiens* (1939) and *The Common Sense of War and Peace* (1940) he stressed, as he had before, the need for a world order and government.

While he was living at Hanover Terrace, one of the great dupes of all time was played on an unsuspecting public, which drew its inspiration from Wells' work. On the evening of 30 October 1938 millions of listeners to the Columbia Broadcasting System radio network in the United States heard that the Martians had landed in New Jersey, and were advancing upon New York — a situation which Wells had created in *The War of the Worlds*, though it seemed that the Martians had chosen New Jersey and New York in preference to leafy Surrey and London. Many of those who had not heard the initial announcement that this was a radio play were genuinely panic-stricken. In fact, the play had been tellingly concocted by Orson Welles, inspired by H.G.Wells' tale. The latter, however, did not see the funny side of what was in a way a complimentary episode, and only belatedly withdrew his threat to sue.

Air raids

Throughout the War Wells stayed doggedly on at Hanover Terrace, sleeping upstairs despite the air raids and refusing invitations to stay with friends in the country. During his last years there, he painted a mural in a room behind the house: a set of panels depicting the story of evolution to the present, it was a grimly pessimistic vision, with the words: 'Time to Go' inscribed beneath the figure of Man.

From 1944 onwards Wells' health slowly deteriorated, and he lived the life of a semi-invalid, seldom venturing out except to walk across the park or to visit the Savile Club. In 1945 he published *Mind at the End of Its Tether*; he lived to see the horrors of Hiroshima, and to have the ironic satisfaction that he had prophesied the atom bomb as early as 1914 in *The World Set Free*. He became increasingly gloomy, feeling more and more that his voice, once respected, was now ignored, and in an article 'The Betterave Papers' published in July 1945, he prophesied (this time inaccurately) what the future's verdict would be on his work:

People whom once he [Wells] had duped would perhaps

mention him as a figure of some significance in English literature, but the established reply of the people who no longer read him and had nothing to say about him, was simply the grimace of those who scent decay. 'Oh, *Wells!*' they would say, and leave it at that.

Wells died at Hanover Terrace on 13 August 1946, at the age of seventy-nine.

13 Hanover Terrace, where Wells stayed throughout the Second World War

John Wesley (1703–91)

47 City Road, EC1

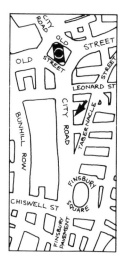

Tube: Old Street.
Bus: Nos. 5, 43, 55, 76, 104, 141, 214, 243, 271.

It was not until he was well into old age that Wesley moved to the City Road. Though he spent much of his time travelling tirelessly up and down the country preaching his beliefs, Methodism greatly needed a focal point for its preaching force in the metropolis. For forty years, Wesley's London headquarters was the Foundry on the edge of Moorfields, where he had preached in the open air to large crowds. The building was a former government arsenal which had blown up, and had been repaired by Wesley, providing a chapel, schools, a book room for Methodist publications, the first free clinic and dispensary in the city, and living space for himself and other preachers.

New headquarters

However, with the expansion of Methodism these quarters soon proved inadequate, and Wesley began to look around for a new site. He issued an appeal for funds and, in April 1777, the building of the City Road Chapel began on a vacant site nearby, followed by that of a house in the forecourt for himself and his assistants. Happily all the buildings have survived — although in 1940 Wesley's house was barely saved during the Blitz by firemen — and both Chapel and House may be visited. The complex of buildings forms a peaceful enclave, hemmed in by office blocks, factories and warehouses, by the side of the busy City Road, which in Wesley's time was described as 'an easy and pleasant communication from the eastern parts of the City to all the roads between Islington and Paddington . . . thus avoiding the necessity of travelling three miles over the stones'. The Chapel was thus easy to get to, and at the same time was on the very fringe of open country. Opposite the House and Chapel, appropriately enough, are Bunhill Fields, the famous cemetery where many of the great non-conformists — including Bunyan, Defoe, Isaac Watts and William Blake — are buried.

The Chapel was opened in November 1778, and Wesley's House was ready the following year. The latter is a tall square house, with four storeys and a basement. Wesley's apartments were on the first floor; his study was at the front of the house, a back room looking out on the Chapel was his bedroom, while he used another small room for private prayer.

Welcome and unwelcome visitors

Many other preachers stayed in this spacious house. Wesley's brother Charles, the famous hymnwriter, was a frequent visitor, and would stay on the second floor; many of his hymns were in fact written here in bursts of inspiration (some of the manuscripts are now displayed in the house). But Wesley's régime with guests was strict, as he recorded in his Journal on 9 December 1787:

> I went down at half-hour past five [in the morning] but found no preacher in the chapel, though we had three or four in the house; so I preached myself. Afterwards, inquiring why none of my family attended the morning preaching, they said it was because they sat up too late. I resolved to put a stop to this; and therefore ordered that everyone under my roof should go to bed at nine.

He does not record whether everyone obeyed!

Not all Wesley's visitors were welcome: being large and new, the house more than once attracted the attention of thieves. In November 1784, Wesley recorded that several men broke into

Wesley's House, 47 City Road, open to the public throughout the year Mon-Sat 10.00-13.00 and 14.00-16.00. The house has recently been beautifully restored, and contains furniture and many personal items which belonged to John and Charles Wesley. (Tel. 01-253 2262)

The small room adjoining John Wesley's bedroom which he used for private prayer

The 'electrical machine', apparently used by Wesley to treat many afflictions including 'melancholia' or depression, is now on display at 47 City Road

the house at three o'clock one morning, and were gathering spoils in the parlour, when:

> just at this time the alarum, which by mistake had [been] set for half past three (instead of four), went off, as it usually did, with a thundery noise. At this the thieves ran away, with all speed, though their work was not half done.

The triumph of Methodism

The years at City Road saw the triumphant expansion of Methodism, its membership more than doubling in the decade 1780–90. Gone were the days when Wesley had faced stoning and ridicule for his open-air preaching; now he was accepted by the establishment, and recorded 'more invitations to preach in churches than I can accept of'. Even in his eighties he worked tirelessly, and continued to go on extensive preaching tours. Crowds would flock to the City Road Chapel to hear him; when numbers were too great, the congregation would cross the road to hear him preach in Bunhill Fields, an area of land (now a public garden) which had long been associated with Nonconformism.

A very different side of Wesley's London life was provided by the intellectual circles in which he was accepted — Doctor Johnson, for instance, found him a congenial companion, but far too taken up with his work, and he complained:

> John Wesley's conversation is good, but he is never at leisure — He is always obliged to go at a certain hour. This is very disagreeable to a man who loves to fold his legs and have his talk out, as I do.

Wesley died at the City Road house in March 1791, at the age of eighty-eight, in his little first-floor bedroom. The day before the burial his open coffin was placed in the Chapel, and ten thousand people filed past it. Wesley is buried in a vault in the ground just east of the apse of the small Foundry Chapel (its name a reminder of the earlier Methodist chapel), where many other early Methodists were buried.

James Abbott McNeill Whistler (1834–1903)

96 Cheyne Walk, SW10

Born in Lowell, Massachusetts, Whistler decided to make London his home in 1859, at the age of twenty-five. Tired of Paris, where he had spent the previous four years studying the work of the great painters of the day, he moved to London and for a while stayed with his sister and brother-in-law at 42 Sloane Street, SW1. Later, perhaps under the influence of Rossetti (who lived at 16 Cheyne Walk), Whistler moved to Chelsea in 1863 and rented no. 101 Cheyne Walk (part of Lindsey House, where the Brunels had also lived earlier in the century). From then until his death Whistler more or less made Chelsea his home, having eight different addresses in the area. It was at 96 Cheyne Walk (also part of Lindsey House), however, that he stayed longest. He moved there in 1866 shortly after his mysterious trip to Valparaiso to support the Chileans in their fight against the Spanish, and lived there until 1878.

Tube: South Kensington.
Bus: Nos. 11, 19, 22, 39, 45, 49.

Personal taste

The twelve years Whistler spent at 96 Cheyne Walk (then no. 2 Lindsey Row) were his most prolific, and probably the happiest period of his career — the growing tide of criticism of his innovative style had not yet embittered him. Whistler decorated the house according to his very personal taste. In complete contrast to the Victorian predilection for rooms cluttered with furniture and bric-à-brac, thick carpets and elaborate wallpapers, Whistler's house had little furniture, plain distempered walls, matting on the floors, and *objets d'art* carefully chosen to complement their surroundings. While in Paris, Whistler had been greatly attracted by Japanese art, and though he was to form a distaste for it after the 1867 Paris Exhibition made it the latest craze, the house contained many 'Japanesisms': purple Japanese fans adorned the walls and ceiling of the blue-painted dining room.

This house was the scene of Whistler's famous 'Sunday breakfasts', to which the artist would invite up to twenty people. They were scheduled to begin at midday, but Whistler would rarely appear before 2 pm. However, his conversation, anecdotes, histrionic wine-pouring and home-made buckwheat cakes invariably soothed his impatient guests. The 'Japanese artist', as he was

96 Cheyne Walk, part of
Lindsey House

known, became a well known local figure and attracted a number
of followers, the first of whom were the brothers Henry and Walter
Greaves, sons of a Chelsea boatman, whom Whistler taught to
paint, so he said, in exchange for rowing lessons.

Paintings of Chelsea

At 96 Cheyne Walk, in his studio at the rear of the second floor,
Whistler produced some of his best portraits, including those of his
mother (who lived with him) and of that other Chelsea resident
Thomas Carlyle, who considered the artist quite mad. Whistler
also executed here several Japanese-inspired canvasses, including
Variations in Blue and Green and *Harmony in Grey and Green*, for
which his model, nine-year-old Cecily Alexander, was made to

Whistler's *Nocturne in Blue and Gold,* one of his impressions of Old Battersea Bridge. *(Tate Gallery)*

endure over seventy sessions, the artist blithely disregarding her tears of boredom. The *Nocturnes* also date from this period. Many of these have the Thames for their subject: either walking by the river or rowed by the Greaves, Whistler would memorize the lights, tones and shapes of a scene, to recreate its atmosphere on canvas on his return to the house. One of his frequent subjects in etchings and paintings was the old wooden-built Battersea Bridge, built in 1771, which then stood near the site of the present bridge. Whistler's paintings and etchings of Chelsea powerfully recreated Chelsea as it was in his early years there, a quiet riverside village, before the Embankment (opened in 1874) distanced the village from the river. Chelsea was to change quite dramatically in the course of Whistler's lifetime.

Despite his prolific output, Whistler frequently suffered financial crises, and usually had to rely on his friend, the not entirely reputable Charles Howell, to bail him out. On one occasion Howell showed particular ingenuity. Whistler was highly puzzled when

Howell returned from the pawnshop, where he had taken a sketch by Whistler of what he thought the planned Brompton Oratory should look like, with a vast sum of money. Some days later Whistler discovered the reason for this sudden windfall: there in the window of the pawnshop was his sketch, labelled 'Michael Angelo's first Drawing for St. Peter's'!

Libel and bankruptcy

Financial problems came to a head when, in July 1877, John Ruskin denounced one of Whistler's *Nocturnes* as a 'pot of paint flung in the public's face'. Whistler sued him for libel and when the case was eventually heard in November 1878 was awarded the derisory sum of one farthing's damages — and ordered to pay his own costs. The blow could not have come at a worse time, as Whistler had just moved to the new house he had built for himself. In the mid 1870s he planned to create his own artistic 'school' and to build a large house in which the plan could be realized. He engaged the architect E.W. Godwin, a site was found in Tite Street, and a three-storey house was designed, with a studio on the top floor, and the 'school' on the second. The White House, as it was called, was so simple in its outside appearance and so unlike anything else in the street, with its white walls and green slate roof, that the Board of Works insisted that decorative mouldings be added, to keep up the tone of the street. But whatever its architectural merits, the expense had been enormous, and faced with the costs of the court case Whistler declared himself bankrupt in May 1879. The following September he left the White House after his short stay, and after climbing a ladder to inscribe above the front door a parting witticism:

> Except the Lord build the house, they labour in vain that build it. E.W. Godwin, F.S.A., built this one.

The house and its contents were auctioned, and Whistler departed for Venice.

By November 1880 he was back in Tite Street at no. 13, near enough to the White House to vent his malice against its new owner (ironically an art critic). He now concentrated less on painting than on cultivating his eccentricity and polishing his wit, largely for verbal battles with another Tite Street resident, Oscar Wilde. Thereafter Whistler travelled frequently, living in Paris for some years after his marriage to E.W. Godwin's widow Beatrix in 1888, and he had a number of London addresses before finally settling in Chelsea, his spiritual home, in 1902, at 74 Cheyne Walk (now demolished), a newly built house on the site of a fish shop. Though he complained violently about the noise of building operations on the house next door, he continued to paint, but his strength was ebbing. He died there on 17 July 1903 and was buried alongside his wife in Chiswick cemetery.

William Wilberforce (1759–1833)

44 Cadogan Place, SW1

Two plaques in London mark the former residences of William
Wilberforce, MP and anti-slavery campaigner. They are at 111
Broomwood Road, Wandsworth and at 44 Cadogan Place in
Chelsea.

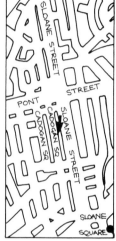

Tube: Sloane Square.
Bus: Nos. 19, 22, 137.

The plaque at Broomwood Road has been erected on a house
on the site of a former house, or houses, where Wilberforce lived
for sixteen years. Broomwood House, where he lived from 1797–
1808, was demolished in 1904, and one of the new houses on the
site was chosen to carry a plaque to commemorate Wilberforce's
association with the area.

Clapham retreat

In the spring of 1792, Wilberforce's close friend Henry Thornton
suggested that Wilberforce and some other friends should move
into his manor house, Battersea Rise. The house was immediately
to the south of Clapham Common, and though Wilberforce
considered the area 'poor mimicry of the real (live) country' he
was happy to move into Thornton's 'communal' household. The
small Queen Anne villa provided a welcome refuge from the busy
premises at 4 Palace Yard, Westminster, where Wilberforce
lived previously, and from the fogs and noise of London. There he
could always be among congenial companions, who included
Wilberforce's great friend William Pitt.

Thornton then built two more houses on the small estate at
Battersea Rise, one of which was named Broomfield Lodge (it
was later renamed Broomwood, in the mid nineteenth century).
When Wilberforce married in 1797, he rented this house from
Edward Eliot, Pitt's brother-in-law; and when Eliot died later
that year, the obvious thing to do was to buy the house from
Eliot's executors.

Wilberforce and his family stayed at Broomfield until 1808. It
was while he was living here that the campaign against slavery,
which he led, reached its climax, in the three years 1804–7. It was
a long struggle: in 1804 the bill to abolish the slave trade passed
the Commons, only to be defeated by the Lords. In 1805 the
Commons defeated the bill on its second reading. Finally, in
1807, the bill passed through both houses.

To Kensington

Having achieved success in outlawing the traffic in slaves, Wilberforce continued to work tirelessly for the total abolition of slavery as well as for a host of other causes. The strain of travelling daily the four miles from Clapham to Westminster eventually became too much for him — his wife wrote of his 'constant state of oscillation between Broomfield and Palace Yard' — so they moved in 1808 to Gore House, Kensington. The Albert Hall now stands on the exact site of this house. For Wilberforce, it made a pleasant change to be able to walk home

44 Cadogan Place, where
Wilberforce died in 1833

from Westminster, though Thornton, who bought 4 Palace Yard from him, noted that Wilberforce would often stay at Palace Yard after working late, and commented wryly that 'Mr Wilberforce I hope has forgotten that Palace Yard is no longer his, for he dines here naturally at any hour except ours'!

Gore House was pleasantly situated: on one side it overlooked Hyde Park and Kensington Gardens beyond, while to the south lay market gardens, where the museums of South Kensington stand today. Again, it was not quite the country, but he could still 'sit and read under the shade . . . with as much admiration of the beauties of nature . . . as if I were two hundred miles from the great city' — in his native Yorkshire, perhaps.

Like Broomfield, Gore House was constantly flooded by streams of well-wishers and fellow campaigners who came to discuss philanthropic projects of all kinds: 'His rooms were filled by crowds which beset his table, and overflowed into his verandah and garden; they came from every quarter, of every creed and tongue.' Meals were usually attended by large numbers of visitors, despite the Wilberforces' reputation for never providing enough to eat: this was due in large measure to Barbara Wilberforce's complete inability to manage the servants employed by her husband, who seem to have been selected, or collected, more for their infirmity or neediness than for competence!

From Gore House, Wilberforce moved in 1821 to Uxbridge, and thence to Highwood Hill near Mill Hill to the north of London on his retirement from politics in 1825. By 1831 his health was deteriorating, and he moved again. He had always loved Bath, visiting the spa several times a year, and now moved permanently to North Parade, a Regency terrace in Bath.

Last days

Now aged seventy-three, in 1833 Wilberforce was stricken with a severe attack of influenza, and in July came up to London to consult a doctor. His cousin, Mrs Lucy Smith, lent him her house, 44 Cadogan Place, Chelsea, and he moved in on 9 July, but the illness proved too much for him and he died there on 29 July. However, he had lived to see the culmination of his life's work: on 26 July the Abolition of Slavery bill passed its third reading in the Commons; as its passage through the Lords this time was certain, slavery had been made illegal. The price which the British government had to pay was high, but that could not mar Wilberforce's delight.

44 Cadogan Place is a late Georgian house, part of the estate built by Henry Holland in the Sloane Square area known as Hans Town, and is one of a row of elegant mansions in that exclusive part of London. The house is little changed since Wilberforce's death, though an extra storey and Italianate stucco ornamentation were added c. 1850.

Oscar Wilde (1854–1900)

34 Tite Street, SW3

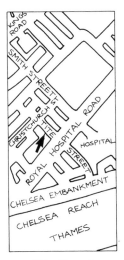

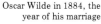

Oscar Wilde in 1884, the
year of his marriage

When Oscar Wilde moved to 34 Tite Street he was thirty years old, and already a well known figure. Since coming to London, the self-styled 'Professor of Aesthetics and Critic of Art' had rapidly become a Society cult, his wit and poetry being given considerable prominence in the Society paper *The World* conveniently edited by Oscar's brother Willie. Now, in 1884, Oscar had decided to marry, and like many others in aesthetic circles had chosen a 'child-bride', whom he described in a letter:

> I am going to be married to a beautiful girl called
> Constance Lloyd, a grave, slight, violet-eyed little Artemis,
> with great coils of heavy brown hair which make her
> flower-like head droop like a blossom. . .

With the aid of Constance's dowry, they were able to pay for the lease on the Tite Street house. They had chosen a fashionable street, favoured by artists because many of the houses had enormous studios, while those at the river end were built high to afford fine views. The Wildes' house, however, was further up the street, and a rather nondescript red brick terrace, with balconies and bay windows through three storeys.

'Good Taste'

However ordinary outside, the house was quickly transformed within. The architect Godwin was engaged to decorate it, and Oscar was naturally anxious to use this opportunity to express his taste to the full. The result was a house with a style all of its own, with some touches of the Oriental, the Pre-Raphaelite, and even the Victorian. As in the White House built for Whistler, Godwin made extensive use of white, at the time a complete novelty in the decorative arts: the white front door opened on to a white hallway and staircase with white matting. Despite Wilde's battle of wits with Whistler, the latter designed the ceiling of the drawing-room, with its crowning touch of two peacock feathers. The dining-room, described proudly by Wilde, was one example of his 'exquisite' taste:

> I have, for instance, a dining-room done in different shades
> of white, with white curtains embroidered in yellow silk:

'The House Beautiful' –
34 Tite Street

the effect is absolutely delightful, and the room is beautiful...

The house was to have great influence, as the practical expression of the chief subject of Wilde's lectures — Good Taste. It was frequently featured in the magazine of which Wilde was editor at this time, *Lady's World*, a Society magazine offering the last word on the fashions of the day. In 1888 Wilde changed its name to *Woman's World*, and did his best to choose the most eminent contributors possible, even requesting some poetic contributions from Queen Victoria, who did not oblige him with a reply. For a while, Wilde was enthusiastic about the venture, commuting daily on the Underground from Sloane Square to Charing Cross and walking from there to the editorial offices at Ludgate Hill. But the mounds of work to be done soon bored him, and he in turn bored the management, who finally sacked him in October 1889. However, his literary career was by this time flourishing in other ways, and in 1891 his *Picture of Dorian Gray* was published followed by a string of successful plays, including *Lady Windermere's Fan* and *A Woman of No Importance*. Oscar's writing was done at Tite Street, in a small study on the ground floor facing the street, where he worked at a table which had belonged to Carlyle.

Proud father

The Wildes lived at Tite Street for eleven years. For a short while, they were devoted to each other. They would frequently be seen strolling the streets of Chelsea in fantastic attire according to Oscar's latest whim of fashion, and once when a local urchin taunted: "Amlet and Ophelia out for a walk I suppose' Wilde replied: 'My little fellow, you are quite right. We are.' Their two children, Cyril and Vyvyan, were born in 1885 and 1886, and Wilde seems to have been a proud father, as Vyvyan recalled:

> He had so much of the child in his nature that he delighted
> in playing our games. He would go down on all fours on
> the nursery floor. . . caring nothing for his normally
> immaculate appearance.

Infatuation

But domestic bliss could not hold Wilde's interest for long. In the early years the House Beautiful in Tite Street had become a *salon*, drawing the aesthetes away from Lady Wilde's *salon* in nearby Oakley Street, where her son had in any event been the star attraction; but the pull of the theatrical world, and Oscar's growing infatuation with Lord Alfred Douglas whom he met in 1891, took his life away from Tite Street. Finally, in 1894, the house was the scene of Wilde's famous showdown with the Marquis of Queensberry, when Wilde, pointing at the Marquis, turned to his servant and said:

> This is the Marquis of Queensberry, the most infamous
> brute in London. You are never to allow him to enter my
> house again.

It was the beginning of the chain of events that led to Wilde's arrest at the Cadogan Hotel, Sloane Street, and his conviction for sodomy and sentence to two years' imprisonment in May 1895. And it was the end of the House Beautiful: the house and its contents were put up for sale, and in the disorder of the auction, which amounted virtually to pillage, many valuable manuscripts were lost or destroyed. Wilde was never to return to Chelsea: after his release from Reading Gaol in 1897 he spent the rest of his life in France and Italy, under an assumed name.

Virginia Woolf (1882–1941)

Hogarth House, Paradise Road, Richmond

Two plaques in London commemorate Virginia Woolf, née Stephen — neither of them, strangely, in Bloomsbury, despite her close association with the Bloomsbury Group.

After the death in 1904 of their brilliant but tempestuous father Sir Leslie Stephen left them parentless, the first house to which Thoby, Vanessa and Virginia Stephen moved was in fact in Bloomsbury. No. 46 Gordon Square was chosen to be as far away as possible from their former family home, 22 Hyde Park Gate (where Leslie Stephen is commemorated by a plaque), and away from anxious relatives in Kensington who were appalled by the move to such an unfashionable neighbourhood. 46 Gordon Square is still standing, and bears a plaque to John Maynard Keynes, who lived there from 1916 until 1946. It is a tall, elegant and roomy house, a typical Bloomsbury nineteenth century terrace.

Tube: Richmond.
Bus: Nos. 33, 37, 71, 73.

Further moves

The first plaque commemorating Virginia Stephen in London adorns 29 Fitzroy Square (earlier occupied by George Bernard Shaw). This is the house to which Virginia and her younger brother Adrian moved in 1907, leaving Vanessa to live at Gordon Square with Clive Bell, whom she had recently married soon after the sudden death of Thoby. Though not in Bloomsbury, the house was within easy reach of their sister's, and they were able to continue at Fitzroy Square the weekly social gatherings which were the genesis of the Bloomsbury Group.

When the lease of this house expired in 1911, they moved again, this time back to Bloomsbury, to 38 Brunswick Square, a huge four-storeyed house which they proceeded to divide up for the use of various friends. One of these 'lodgers' was Leonard Woolf: he and Virginia quickly became close, and were married on 10 August 1912.

Richmond

It was after the return from their honeymoon, when Virginia

undertook the final revision of her first novel, *The Voyage Out*, that she suffered from the most serious mental breakdown of her life, that was to last intermittently for two years and, like her later breakdowns, characteristically occurred during the final stages of writing one of her 'visionary' novels. However, during one of the more lucid periods of her illness, early in 1915, when she and Leonard were lodging in Richmond with a view to finding a home out of the centre of London, they came across, and fell in love with, Hogarth House. At the time, Hogarth House was one half of a large, semi-detached residence built of brick, dating from c. 1748, which had been divided into two houses, the eastern (right-hand) portion being known as Hogarth House and the other as Suffield House. (Since restoration in 1971–72, the whole building has been known as Hogarth House.) Despite delays and difficulties in obtaining the lease, Leonard Woolf finally succeeded, and in March 1915 the Woolfs made Hogarth House their new home.

Partly for pleasure and partly to aid Virginia's slow and painful recovery, the Woolfs decided, on her thirty-third birthday, to buy themselves a printing press, and to take up printing as a hobby. Subsequently they found, in a small printing shop in Farringdon Street near Holborn Viaduct, a small handpress, which they bought with all the necessary equipment for under twenty pounds. They set to work immediately the press arrived at Hogarth House, Virginia setting the type, frequently upside down, Leonard painstakingly correcting it and operating the press. Their first effort was a thirty-two page booklet, priced at 1s.6d., consisting of two stories, one each of Leonard's and Virginia's. As it turned out, this relaxing pastime was eventually to become a professional and profitable business, publishing many of the most well known works of the 1920s, including T.S. Eliot's *The Waste Land* — quickly past were the days of the old handpress.

The Hogarth Press

Increasingly also Virginia saw the advantages of publishing her own work without having to bow to the demands of other, possibly unsympathetic publishers. Thus, after her second novel, *Night and Day*, was published in 1919, all her work was published by the Hogarth Press, including *Kew Gardens* and *Monday or Tuesday*, written at Hogarth House. Meanwhile, in the summer of 1919, they had found a new country home, Monk's House, in the village of Rodmell near Lewes in Sussex, and here Virginia was to do much of her writing.

Eventually, in 1924, the Woolfs moved from Hogarth House back to Bloomsbury. Life at Hogarth House, after Virginia's recovery, had been happy and peaceful, a round of writing in the morning, walking in the afternoon and reading in the evening,

Hogarth House,
Richmond, where the
Woolfs began The Hogarth
Press

with the occasional trip to central London. But Virginia was
increasingly anxious to return to the active social life to which
she had been accustomed before her breakdown, and though
worried as to the effect this would have on her mental health,
Leonard agreed to move back when Virginia found and took the
lease of no. 52 Tavistock Square. Here they continued to run
the Hogarth Press from the basement, and occupied the top two
floors, renting the ground and first floors to a firm of solicitors.
The house, now demolished, continued to be their London
home until 1939, two years before Virginia's suicide.

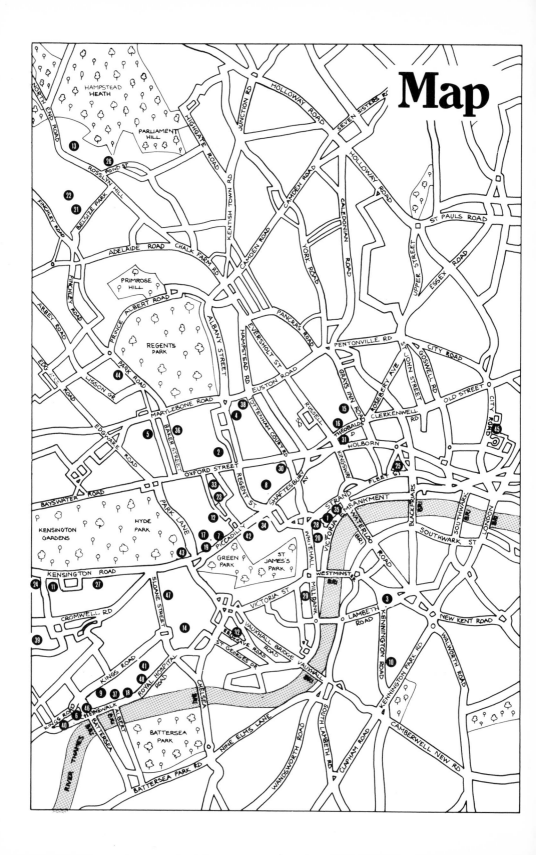

Map

Map references

1 **Robert Adam** 1-3 Robert Street, WC2
2 **Hector Berlioz** 58 Queen Anne Street, W1
3 **William Bligh** 100 Lambeth Road, SE1
4 **James Boswell** 122 Great Portland Street, W1
5 **Elizabeth Barrett Browning** 99 Gloucester Place, W1
6 **Isambard Kingdom Brunel** 98 Cheyne Walk, SW10
7 **Fanny Burney** 11 Bolton Street, W1
8 **Antonio Canaletto** 41 Beak Street, W1
9 **Thomas Carlyle** 24 Cheyne Row, SW3
10 **Charlie Chaplin** 287 Kennington Road, SE11
11 **Sir Winston Churchill** 28 Hyde Park Gate, SW7
12 **Robert, Lord Clive** 45 Berkeley Square, W1
13 **John Constable** 40 Well Walk, NW3
14 **Noel Coward** 17 Gerald Road, SW1
15 **Charles Dickens** 48 Doughty Street, WC2
16 **Benjamin Disraeli** 22 Theobalds Road, WC1
17 **Benjamin Disraeli** 19 Curzon Street, W1
18 **George Eliot** 4 Cheyne Walk, SW3
19 **Charles James Fox** 46 Clarges Street, W1
20 **Benjamin Franklin** 36 Craven Street, WC2
21 **Sigmund Freud** 20 Maresfield Gardens, NW3
22 **Kate Greenaway** 39 Frognal, NW3
23 **Georg Friedrich Handel** 25 Brook Street, W1
24 **Henry James** 34 De Vere Gardens, W8
25 **Samuel Johnson** 17 Gough Square, EC4
26 **John Keats** Keats' House, Keats Grove, NW3
27 **John F. Kennedy** 14 Princes Gate, SW7
28 **Rudyard Kipling** 43 Villiers Street, WC2
29 **T.E. Lawrence** 14 Barton Street, SW1
30 **Karl Marx** 28 Dean Street, W1
31 **William Morris** 17 Red Lion Square, WC1
32 **Wolfgang Amadeus Mozart** 180 Ebury Street, SW1
33 **Horatio, Viscount Nelson** 103 New Bond Street, W1
34 **Sir Isaac Newton** 87 Jermyn Street, SW1
35 **Samuel Pepys** 12 Buckingham Street, WC2
36 **William Pitt** 120 Baker Street, W1
37 **Robert Falcon Scott** 56 Oakley Street, SW3
38 **George Bernard Shaw** 29 Fitzroy Square, W1
39 **Ellen Terry** 22 Barkston Gardens, SW5
40 **J.M.W. Turner** 119 Cheyne Walk, SW10
41 **Mark Twain** 23 Tedworth Square, SW3
42 **Horace Walpole** 5 Arlington Street, SW1
43 **Duke of Wellington** Apsley House, 149 Piccadilly, W1
44 **H.G. Wells** 13 Hanover Terrace, NW1
45 **John Wesley** 47 City Road, EC1
46 **James Abbott McNeill Whistler** 96 Cheyne Walk, SW10
47 **William Wilberforce** 44 Cadogan Place, SW1
48 **Oscar Wilde** 34 Tite Street, SW3

Acknowledgements

Acknowledgements are due to the following for permission to reproduce illustrative material: Her Majesty The Queen; Magdalene College, Cambridge; the National Gallery; the National Trust; Robert Douwma Prints & Maps Ltd, London; St Martin's Prints, London; the Tate Gallery; the Victoria and Albert Museum; the National Portrait Gallery, for permission to use all the portraits, except that of Dickens on page 52; and Swiss Cottage Library, for the sketches reproduced on pages 21, 46, 52, 118 and 134. Thanks are also due to the Trustees of Dr Johnson's House for allowing us to photograph at 17 Gough Square; to Douglas Wollen and Max Woodward for much kind advice and information on Wesley's House; to the Greater London Council for access to their Blue Plaque files; to Jill Parker of London Transport for supplying information on bus routes; and to Scott Raeburn and Neil Wenborn for copy-editing and proof-reading respectively. I would particularly like to thank the photographers: Helen Douglas-Cooper, for the house photographs on pages 40, 48, 73, 77, 78, 91, 120, 125, 127, 131, 133, 157; and Sandy Young, for the photographs on pages 11, 12, 15, 18, 20, 23, 27, 30, 34, 37, 42, 45, 51, 54, 55, 57, 61, 63, 65, 68, 71, 80, 82, 83, 84, 87, 93, 95, 96, 97, 100, 105, 108, 110, 113, 117, 122, 129, 135, 138, 141, 143, 144, 146, 150 and 153, and who also drew all the maps. Finally, I would like to thank Chris Mann, for asking me to write this book, and for the information contained in his *Where the Famous Lived in London*; and Mike Edwards and Dave Young, for all their efforts in putting this book together.